Operating Under C

The Life and Work of Arthur Clar
Consultant Surgeon at the Jersey General Hospital
During the German Occupation, 1940-1945

Written and compiled by Michael Halliwell

Published by:
Channel Islands Occupation Society (Jersey)

May, 2005

To my wife, Susan, for her loving support and encouragement over many years;
my children Katharine, Philip, Elisabeth, David, Rachel;
and my grandchildren, Stephen, Matthew, Anna, Michael, Helen, Nikolai,
Thomas, Gethin, William, Chloë, Barnaby,
in all of whom the future rests.

Foreword

By Sir Peter Crill KBE
Bailiff of Jersey 1986-1995

To write a foreword about someone who, sixty years ago, was regarded in medical circles as a demi-god is difficult enough, but when one's main contact was a professional one in 1937 it makes the task, however agreeable, somewhat difficult. I must therefore do as Michael did and rely on what people over the years have told me.

There is no doubt that Arthur Halliwell was one of the most dedicated and brilliant surgeons to work in Jersey. Side by side with his official life, until disrupted by the Occupation in 1940, he was a devoted family man and led an idyllic life, which Michael's recollection brings out very clearly. In common with hundreds of others in that terrible year of evacuation he had to make a difficult choice and he decided to remain in the Island, having sent his family away. It was fortunate for the General Hospital that he remained because there is no doubt that his sense of discipline kept it going. This is not to say that he couldn't get on with people or was not capable of warmth but he could be somewhat quirky. Who can blame him? Everyone's personality was put under a great strain and tested as never before. His innovations when some medical supplies were practically nil undoubtedly saved many patients' lives. I broke both bones in my right leg in 1937 and Mr. Halliwell – I could never think of him as anything else – set the leg but warned me that I might have arthritis in later life. So well had he done his job that at least in the leg I've no trace of it. Apart from this, when I escaped from the Island in 1944 Mr. Halliwell very kindly conveyed our outboard motor to the embarkation site at no little risk to himself.

Arthur Halliwell worked closely with the Medical Officer of Health, Dr. McKinstry, and our own family doctor, Harold John Blampied, who wore himself out so that he died not long after the Occupation, and in 1952 his name was included on the Victoria College War memorial. A remarkable, dedicated and efficient triumvirate, they were assisted most ably by Dr. Averell Darling.

A good deal of the story told by Michael concerns the doings of the Halliwell clan, but he has given an insight into life during the Occupation which is remarkably accurate for someone who wasn't there, and I have no doubt that he remembered what his father had told him. After the Liberation the Bailiff and other officials received well merited honours. It remains a scandal that Arthur Halliwell was not among the recipients, but this account will surely serve to keep his memory alive for all who knew him and remind future generations of one who served our Island with such dedication.

Jersey, March 2005

Operating Under Occupation

The Life and Work of Arthur Clare Halliwell FRCS,
Consultant Surgeon at the Jersey General Hospital
During the German Occupation, 1940-1945

Written and compiled by Michael Halliwell

Editor:
Matthew Costard B A (Hons)

Artwork and Production:
Dave Williams

Published by:
Channel Islands Occupation Society (Jersey)
'Les Geonnais de Bas', Rue des Geonnais,
St. Ouen, Jersey JE3 2BS.

Fly Sheet: Arthur Clare Halliwell FRCS, as a Surgeon Lieutenant in 1918.

Back cover: A graphic painting by local artist, Gerald Palmer, which depicts the bombing attack by Heinkel III aircraft of Luftflotte 3 on St. Helier Harbour, on 28th June 1940.
Painting photographed by Robin Briault, and reproduced by kind permission of the artist and the Jersey War Tunnels.

ISBN 0 9550086 0 3

Contents

Contents (Continued)

Introduction

The idea for this book, originally intended for my family, came when my brother Anthony drew my attention to a book written by an Irish nurse who had served at the Jersey General Hospital in the early part of the Second World War. In it she gave a number of pen portraits of our father, Arthur Clare Halliwell, then a consultant surgeon there.

Subsequently, my brother told me of another autobiographical account by one of his patients, also containing some memorable descriptions of him at work in the Hospital. Here, he was being brought to life by two people who vividly remembered him. As children of a prominent person we really only saw him as a father; we were aware of his professional skills, but we could not see him as others saw him.

He had come to Jersey shortly before his marriage to our mother, Winifred Dorothea Goode, and joined the staff of the General Hospital as Consultant Surgeon in 1932. I was born in 1928, my brother Anthony in 1930, my sister Daphne in 1933, and my brother Richard in 1937.

I wanted to share this with the rest of the family and so conceived the idea of collecting extracts from these two books and interviewing people who had worked with my father or had memories of him. I then had a collection of reminiscences. Next, I needed some background to the story, so I turned to the many books written on Occupation experiences, of the sufferings and ingenuity of the local people. Obviously, one has to be selective and I have chosen material which, by and large, touched my father's life or ours, whether directly or indirectly. The result is inevitably something of a patchwork, but there is really no other way of documenting a period of history which was as complex as the Occupation.

The letters which our parents exchanged just before and immediately after the Occupation are a valuable insight into what they were experiencing, as are the brief Red Cross letters with which they managed to keep in touch and conduct some family business in cryptic form.

Then I realised that all this would need to be placed within the context of the European political scene of the twentieth century. This meant filling the story out with details which are totally familiar to my contemporaries but less familiar to our children, let alone our grandchildren. And I wanted to tell the story, as fully and honestly as possible, with its positive sides, and its negative ones, without exaggeration or diminution.

When, in 1947, I went with my fellow Oxford students to Bonn University in the Rhineland to begin the process of the reconciliation of our two nations, I was completely overawed as I walked through the total devastation of the once proud city of Cologne and saw the remaining inhabitants eking out a living amongst the ruins. One evening, at the Aloysiuskolleg in Bad Godesberg, as the evening sun shone on the Petersberg where Chamberlain had held his abortive meeting with Hitler, we were addressed by Robert Birley, the Educational Adviser to the British Zone of Germany.

He imbued us with a burning enthusiasm to play our part in helping to build a new and peaceful Europe and to help the rising German generation to feel part of the family of nations.

The following afternoon we met some of the university professors in the garden of the college. We carelessly smoked our army issue cigarettes, and ground the stubs into the gravel. When we had finished, these elderly men and women knelt on the ground, opened their silver tobacco boxes and carefully picked up our dog ends. How far had this once proud nation fallen!

Then I came to look at all that the war had done to me and others in the light, not so much of past sufferings, as of future prospects. My predecessors had fought and won a bitter war, and, although trained to fight, I never had to fire a shot in anger. I saw it as my task to help ensure that it could never happen again.

When, some twenty years after my first visit, I returned to Germany as Chaplain to the British Embassy in Bonn, and saw the blue European flag with the twelve gold stars flying on the ferries across the Rhine, it seemed like the end of a nightmare and the fulfilment of a dream.

Hence, another concern of mine was to humanise the people in the story who are so often depicted in negative stereotypes. War attempts to dehumanise the enemy, but peacetime demands another approach. So many of the contemporary accounts, inevitably perhaps, reflect wartime attitudes and are framed in wartime jargon. There are very few accounts from the German side, but one exception is the secret diary of Baron von Aufsess. If I have given what may seem a disproportionate amount of space to this, my excuse is that it is, in my view, a unique account of a person struggling to come to terms with the kind of impossible situation which the war placed on so many.

I have tried to bring out the problem which many local people faced, particularly those in the Jersey Government, of distinguishing between co-operation (necessary to survive) and collaboration (assisting the enemy). The line between these two is extremely hard to draw, and the ultimate judgement of history may be kinder than it was in the heat and immediate aftermath of the conflict.

I have also tried to show from extracts and references to the German doctors, soldiers, and clergy, something of how it seemed to them to be in the grip of a ruthless dictatorship, and of what they did to attempt to oppose or mitigate the evils of a regime which they too had increasingly come to detest.

When, in 1995, we celebrated the 50th anniversary of the Liberation, a German acquaintance, who had formerly served here and was a keen member of the Channel Islands Occupation Society, booked a holiday in a local hotel. I asked him why he had come at this particular time, when we were celebrating Germany's defeat. He replied: "Because it was my liberation too!"

Many of our friends have long regretted the absence of an account of my father's work in the Occupation, and I hope that these reminiscences will help them, my own family, and future generations to know something of the life of a remarkable man in a remarkable period of Island and world history.

Acknowledgements

I am enormously grateful to the many people who have contributed to the appearance of this book. I am largely indebted to Michael Ginns and Matthew Costard of the Channel Islands Occupation Society (Jersey) for agreeing to publish it, and for their invaluable help in assuring accuracy of the text and preparing the manuscript and photographs for publication. Many who lived through these times have contributed, either by sharing (sometimes painful) memories, or by giving permission for me to reproduce material from books they have written concerning the Occupation. Mrs. Yvette Stamberg helped me greatly with corrections and encouragement.

My grateful thanks are due to Sir Peter Crill KBE for kindly agreeing to write the foreword.

The following have been most generous with their time in sharing their stories and/or knowledge:

Nancy Alexandre (née O'Neill), Baron Hans von Aufsess, Donald Bell, Mavis Blampied (née Wills), Pastor Wilhelm Burkert, Elise Cathro (née Floyd), Dr. Averell Darling, Lorna du Pré (née Mackintosh), Dr. Peter Falla, Alastair Fairlie, John and Carette Floyd, Michael Ginns MBE, Audrey Goodwin (née Lock), Leo Harris, Mary Herold (née Blampied), Sidney Horman, Margaret Hunt, George Kozloff, Ernst Kämpfer, Philip Le Cuirot, Daphne Le Marquand, Bob Le Sueur, Mary Le Sueur (née Jouny), Margaret Perkins (née Le Maistre), Xavier Peyre, Kenneth Podger, Colin Powell, Canon Kenneth Preston, Marion Sutton (née Michel), Simone Rogon, Ted Single, and Betty Thurban, who has also contributed much helpful advice.

The following works have also been consulted and I am grateful to those who have given permission for extracts to be included in this book:

BBC Radio Jersey for permission to reproduce material from broadcasts.

Peggy Boléat, *A Quiet Place*, Villette Publishing, 1993.

The Revd Geoffrey Baker, extracts from a sermon.

The Channel Islands Occupation Society (Jersey), extracts from articles.

W.S. Churchill, *History of the Second World War*, Cassell, 1948.

The Memoirs of Lord Coutanche by H. R. S. Pocock, published in 1975 by Phillimore & Co Ltd, Shopwyke Manor Barn, Chichester, West Sussex, PO20 2BG, reproduced by kind permission.

Charles Cruikshank, *The German Occupation of the Channel Islands*, Guernsey Press, 1975.

Val Garnier, *Medical History of the Jersey Hospitals and Nursing Homes during the Occupation 1940-1945*, London, 2002.

Ambrose Greenaway, *A Century of Cross Channel Passenger Ferries*, 1981, by kind permission of Ian Allan Publishing.

Vera Hansford, for the poem, *Male Flat*.

John Herbert MBE, unpublished manuscript, Société Jersiaise.

Donald Journeaux, *Raise the White Flag*, Leatherhead, 1995, permission sought.

Frank Keiller, *Prison Without Bars*, Seaflower, 2000.

John Lewis, *A Doctor's Occupation*, Corgi Books 1982, by kind permission of Penton Lewis and CI Publishing.

Joe Mière, *Never to be Forgotten*, CI Publishing, 2004.

Dr. R. Osmont, manuscript of a talk given to the Société Jersiaise.

Gabriel Rosenstock, kind permission for extracts from *Hello, Is It All Over?* by Mauyen Keane, Ababúna, 1984.

Dr. Paul Sanders, extracts from *The Ultimate Sacrifice*, Jersey Museums Service, 1998, permission sought.

Mrs. Gill Thomas, extracts from *Lest We Forget* by Roy Thomas, La Haule Books, Jersey, 1992.

Richard Weithley, extracts from *So It Was*, Starlight Publishing, 2001.

John Sinel, kind permission for extracts from *The German Occupation of Jersey*, by Leslie Sinel, Evening Post, 1946.

The von Aufsess Occupation Diary translated by K. Nowlan, published in 1985 by Phillimore & Co Ltd, Shopwyke Manor Barn, Chichester, West Sussex, PO20 2BG, reproduced by kind permission.

For permission to reproduce the images in this book, I am indebted to the following organisations: the Société Jersiaise, the Bundesarchiv (who own the copyright for the photographs under reference numbers 101I/228/336/19, 101I/228/333/34 & 101II MW/5143/22A, appearing on pages 88, 121 and 123), Health and Social Services, the Jersey War Tunnels and the Jersey Evening Post.

The following individuals have been particularly helpful: Gareth Syvret (Photographic Archivist, Société Jersiaise), Frau Berit Pistora (Bundesarchiv), Mike Le Fèvre (Director of Estates, Health and Social Services), and Chris Addy (Archivist, Jersey War Tunnels).

I am also most grateful to Betty Thurban, Gabriel Rosenstock and Michael Ginns, who have allowed me to use personal photographs, and to Alan Blampied and the Blampied family for permission to reproduce the portrait of Canon Cohu by Edmund Blampied.

Despite digital manipulation, the quality of some photographs is not as high as we would have wished. However, we felt that their historical value outweighed other considerations.

Chapter 1
1939 - 1940
Phoney War to Blitzkrieg

The story begins early in 1940, as the *Luftwaffe* is preparing for its onslaught on the West and members of the Long Range Reconnaissance Group (123) are waiting, as they said, "in the cafés and at the tram stops of the German catholic city of Cologne."

At the beginning of 1933 Adolf Hitler had been appointed Chancellor of the German State. In March that year the Nazi party won 43% of the vote in national elections and swiftly began implementing measures which were designed to curb individual freedom. Within a month Jewish businesses were being boycotted; in May the Trade Unions were disbanded and in June and July political parties were dissolved. The way was open for the totalitarian state. Universal conscription was introduced in 1935, and by May of the following year over seven thousand people were in prison for political offences.

Hitler began making territorial demands. In March, 1936 German troops re-occupied the demilitarised Rhineland, sending a shockwave through the international community. In November, 1937 Hitler completed secret plans for the annexation of Austria and Czechoslovakia. A year later Austria was annexed to the *Reich*, and Hitler laid claims before the international community for the Sudetenland, those parts of Czechoslovakia inhabited by German speaking populations, as a prelude to annexing the whole country. In September, 1938 the Munich conference granted the Sudetenland to Germany and the British Prime Minister Chamberlain returned to Croydon Airport waving a piece of paper and announcing: "Peace for our time." When it became clear that Hitler was turning further east in his territorial ambitions, Britain and France gave an undertaking that, in the event of a German attack on Poland, they would declare war on Germany. In March, 1939 he took over the rest of Czechoslovakia and on 1st September he invaded Poland. In less than a month Warsaw surrendered. Britain and France, in accordance with their treaty obligations, went to the aid of Poland and declared war.

Winston Churchill once memorably described Adolf Hitler as "a monstrous product of former wrongs." Former wrongs there certainly were, particularly in the aftermath of the First World War. But since the coming to power of the National Socialists in Germany the people had been carefully nurtured on a diet of misinformation, preparing them for the coming conflict. First, Hitler built on the sense of resentment about the aftermath of the defeat in 1918 and secondly, he concocted a diet of anti-Semitism which blamed the Jews for many of Germany's ills. The German people were also constantly fed a tissue of lies concerning the supposedly warlike intentions of neighbouring countries.

In a broadcast to the German people on the day following the outbreak of war Chamberlain attempted to put the record straight, though it is doubtful if many of the German people would have heard the broadcast. Chamberlain concluded:

Your Leader is now sacrificing you, the German people, to the still more monstrous gamble of a war to extricate himself from the impossible position into which he has led himself and you.

In this war we are not fighting against you, the German people, for whom we have no bitter feeling, but against a tyrannous and forsworn regime which has betrayed not only its own people but the whole of Western civilisation and all that you and we hold dear.

May God defend the right!

Prophetic words, but the spirit in which they were written was soon forgotten, and six bloody years of war and millions of deaths were to follow before the German people were to be able to see the truth of these words, and to join with the rest of their European partners in rebuilding our shattered European civilisation.

The first few months of the war saw very little activity. The British Expeditionary Force, including my uncle Christopher Goode, a Driver with the Royal Army Service Corps, landed in France to share in the defence of that country. The French and British armies dug in in defensive positions and Royal Air Force activity was restricted to attacks on German shipping and the dropping of leaflets. It was therefore dubbed "The Phoney War".

Meanwhile, in the Rhineland, around Cologne, the *Luftwaffe* were training for their assault on the West, and on 10th May the *Blitzkrieg* was launched, with lightning speed. *Das Jahr der eisernen Schicksalswende* is the title of a piece of doggerel verse written in 1940 by a German airman for a squadron magazine. This poem is a vivid account of the events of that remarkable campaign and of the role of the 2nd Squadron (Richthofen) Long Range Reconnaissance Group 123 '2./*Aufklärungsgruppe* 123 *(Fern)'* in the subjugation of Belgium, Holland and France in six weeks.

The Group was formed in Würzburg in 1939 and equipped with Dornier *Do17*P, a long range reconnaissance version of the famous "flying pencil" bomber. On 10th May 1940 they flew west and accompanied the victorious German forces through France.

On 30th June one of their aircraft was on a routine reconnaissance flight over Guernsey and decided to land. Very early the next day they dropped the surrender ultimatum over Jersey and later the same day landed at Jersey Airport. The first to arrive on the Island, the unit remained there for eight months.

Dr. John Lewis, a general practitioner recently arrived in Jersey, describes these young men in his book, *A Doctor's Occupation*:

They were very young, many very good looking, impeccably tailored, insufferably arrogant and carried themselves as if they belonged to an entirely different race from the ground troops.

The poem, which bears this out, is quoted in full on the following page.

The Year of the Turn of the Iron Hinge of Fate

The squadron stood ready and fully prepared.
As the heroes' hour grew to full flood
In the Lord God's finest catholic city.
The year began with endless waiting
Waiting at tram stops, in the brightest sun
Waiting to turn on enemy land.
Exercises ordered in heavy snow,
A German road dam damaged by bombs,
From the air alongside the fire was tremendous,
And at evening the throats were fully replenished,
All in all we made good use of the time
Stood fully prepared and ready for off.
As day dawned on the tenth of May -
We were the first to take to the air.
We burst through Belgium's fortress gate
Over the Albert Canal, Eben-Emael, and onwards
Flooded the victorious German army.
We chased the Tommy back over the sea
And in six hot and battle-filled weeks
We broke Belgium, Holland and France.
Over the Dyle-defence, the Maginot Ring.
Unstoppable we flooded onwards,
We destroyed the enemy in the land of Flanders
We ran right through the Weygand line
And always, and ever, with death and destruction
Richthofen was there with his avenging Corps
By roadsides unending throughout the land
So many lay under the green sward.
Finally, victorious on English soil
We were there, Richthofen's reconnaissance fliers.
Haneffe, Charleville, Laon, Soissons, Romilly, Ouilly,-le Tesson -
We'd come a long way through enemy land
And there we were, on the happy Jersey strand.
With plotting and planning the flying was tough
And we danced and danced till we'd had enough.
My son, it began in the Café Wien,
It ended, you know, in West Park Pavilion
And next you will see, we have in our sight
To be dancing victorious on the Isle of Wight.

Chapter 2
The Crisis Approaches

In 1933 my father had taken me to look at a field in St. Peter where he was considering building a family home. Looking at the empty furrows stretching into the distance down a gentle slope towards the sea, and St. Aubin's Bay, I found it hard to imagine what it would be like when the house was completed. On 28th October contract was passed before the Royal Court for the sale of the field by local farmer J.B. Michel for £1,653. A magnificent house, with seven bedrooms, designed in Spanish style by architect C. Boulton, was completed two years later, at the final cost of £5,411.10s.3d. A splendid garden, with terraced lawns falling away into the distance, and an impressive rock garden, were designed by Lawrence Ogilvie of Bristol. An abundance of trees, shrubs, plants and superb flowering cherries was planted, and the retaining walls and foundations for a tennis court were built, the hardcore for the surface consisting mainly of clinker from the Esse cooker. Much of the stonework for the retaining walls was done by my father himself. This garden was to be the scene of countless games of cricket, tennis, birthday parties, some skiing, my youngest brother Richard's memorable twenty-first birthday party, and my own proposal of marriage.

On our Island of Jersey, as the crisis was developing on the Continent, we all felt that the great French Maginot line, built along the frontier between Germany and France was protection enough, and how wrong we were! However, in 1938, during the "Munich Crisis", the States of Jersey had had the foresight to lay in two years' supply of the most commonly used drugs for use in the Hospital.

In a paper written after the war, to which I shall refer from time to time, my father explains how the authorities had prepared the Hospital for war:

When the war started we were very well stocked. It had been decided that we should have a complete spare set of hospital equipment in case we lost ours during air raids, and this was drawn upon as necessary. All the drugs and dressings we had lasted two to three years.

Outwardly all was peaceful - 1940 had begun calmly and life went on as usual. In March, Jersey was advertised in the English papers as "the ideal resort for wartime holidays this summer."

In September, 1939, at the outbreak of war, our parents were aged 43; I was 11, my brother Anthony 9, my sister Daphne 6, and my brother Richard 2. Because of the risk involved in crossing the Channel, and the fact that our school was in Sussex, dangerously close to the scene of conflict, Anthony and I did not return to our boarding school for the autumn term; instead, with children of friends of our parents, we went to lessons with a local tutor.

The year 1940 began with unusually cold weather, and there was skating on Goose Green Marsh, just below our house. My brother went regularly to music lessons and I to French lessons. Our social life continued much as before, a way of life which, though no one could possibly guess it, was shortly to disappear - forever.

There were lots of parties: on 4th January a very big party at St. Helier's West Park Pavilion. In my diary I noted the presence of our friends, Ray Fairlie, Wyshe Read, our neighbours, and Patsy Pallot. The *Evening Post* reported:

The second children's party held yesterday at West Park Pavilion proved eminently successful, there being over three hundred children present and they romped and played all over the ballroom and 'a good time was had by all'. Syd Britton's band was in good form and musical games, dances, not forgetting Boomps-a-Daisy and Palais Glide, made the time pass all too quickly both before and after the tea interval.

There was a lavish tea of cakes, jellies and ices and these quickly disappeared and the children lost no time in getting back on the dance floor. Competitions were won by Pat Pallot, Michael Halliwell, Valerie Ogden and John Harvey for the Palais Glide and by Peter Blampied and Pat Burke for the Musical Bumps. There was, of course, a visit from Father Christmas. [Actually, my prize was for 'Boomps-a-Daisy'!]

Little did we know what the future held in store for us. Before the year was out, we would be evacuated to England; while Jean, Patsy and their families remained to face five years of occupation; and a couple of years later, Wyshe and her family would be deported to Germany.

In two years, instead of doing Boomps-a-Daisy, I would be doing military drill, field craft, map reading and weapons training in my school Officers Training Corps.

The next day there was a dancing class, and on 11th January another party - at de Gruchy's restaurant in St. Helier. I recorded that it was all dancing, and that we had "a super dinner, with lots and lots to eat, and got back very late." Then followed heavy snow and by 19th January we were blowing up balloons for Anthony's tenth birthday party. The party was next day, Saturday, and after morning school we spent the afternoon clearing the drawing room of furniture and carpets. The party began with tea at 4.00 pm, and most of the guests were in fancy dress, with our two friends next door, Jean and Ray, coming as Burmese ladies. The band arrived during tea and we had a long party which finally ended just before 7.30.

On 21st March we had a visit from a naval officer who turned up at the door. I recorded in my diary, "After tea Dr. Eccles RN arrived, resplendent in uniform with gold bands etc." He explained that he had served with my father in the Navy, and they had last met at Portsmouth in 1916. He added that he was now stationed at Jersey Airport with the Fleet Air Arm, and told us that they would be night flying. I added in the diary, "So we watched them when it was dark, but could not see much." Dr. Eccles's visit was to prove providential in the years ahead, for his name was to be used as a code word with which my father could communicate to my mother certain pieces of information which the German censors would not pass if they had known its import.

John Herbert, the Airport Manager, in an unpublished account, gives an interesting view of some of these operations:

I think that it was in February 1940 that we had a Fleet Air Arm Training Squadron based at the Airport under the Command of Lt-Comdr. Mortimer equipped with Swordfish and Albacore aircraft. They set up a torpedo range in St. Ouen's Bay and carried out simulated deck landings at the Airport at night.

As the German Forces overran France and came close to the Channel Islands we were instructed to obstruct the Landing Area before nightfall. We borrowed ploughs, harrows and tractors from neighbouring farmers, also using our own vehicles and equipment, and made a planned obstruction chart. Each item had to be recorded when placed in position and checked in the morning to ensure that it had been removed. One morning we forgot a harrow and by sheer bad luck a Swordfish ran over it on take-off. The Lt-Comdr. was not amused. The Officer in Command of the Cadets stationed at St. Peter's Barracks offered the assistance of two Cadets per evening to help place out the obstructions which I gladly accepted. One evening the Duty Lorry Driver was taken ill and could not report for duty so I drove the lorry myself to collect the cadets. They were in the back of the lorry when I left the barracks. After stopping at the first obstruction point I got out of the lorry and could see no sign of my two cadets. On a careful inspection I found them clinging underneath the lorry's chassis.

Life at home carried on as usual. Lessons, rambles and walks, playing in our huge garden, card games and games with model soldiers. We also helped in the garden, I with mowing the grass. Then, on 21st April when Anthony and I got home from singing in St. Matthew's Church choir, our sister, Daphne announced: "Money going!", and explained that our father was offering one penny (1d) for every dandelion head which we picked. We set to work with a will, so much so that he reduced the piece work rate to $^1/_2$d per head. In the event we picked 1,240, divided up as follows: Anthony 480, Daphne 436, myself 300, and Richard (not yet 3 years old) 24.

Suddenly, at 3.00 am, on 10th May the German *Blitzkrieg* turned west. Their forces subdued Belgium and Holland in five days, drove the British Expeditionary Force to the sea at Dunkirk, and swept down towards Paris.

My twelfth birthday party, held the following day, was a more modest affair than that of my brother. Our guests arrived after lunch, and we began with a game of cricket, my father having put up some very effective netting around the garden to protect his plants. Then we had a treasure hunt, and after tea played the game 'French and English'. With the camera given me by my parents I took a picture of my father relaxing after lunch which we kept with us right through the Occupation.

On Sunday, 26th May, in the face of the crisis facing the whole of Western Europe, the nation united in a National Day of Prayer. Anthony and I went in the morning to St. Matthew's Church, which was full, and in the evening with both our parents to the service at St. Mark's, which was packed to the doors.

All on the Western Front Allied troops were in retreat. Our uncle, Driver Christopher Goode, took part in that desperate march to the sea. He crossed Belgium in convoy, along roads littered with corpses, the stench rising as they decayed in the sun. Their movements were seriously hampered by the large numbers of civilians, with all their bags and baggage, trying to escape from the advancing Germans. They were bombed all the way, and in between snatched a few hours of sleep underneath their lorry, which was loaded with explosives. On reaching the Dunkirk beach Christopher was amazed to see that they were not forgotten, and that every sort of craft had come to their rescue. Even fishing boats and rowing boats were there; some coming right inshore to pick up their human cargo.

Ships which had formerly served the Channel Islands took part in the rescue: the *Isle of Guernsey*, fitted out as a hospital ship, brought back 836 wounded, and the *St. Helier* rescued 10,200 troops and 1,500 refugees, shooting down a German aircraft with her deck gun; sadly, both the *Lorina* and *Normannia* were bombed and sunk.

Not everyone could get away and Christopher felt deeply torn between the need to get back to England and the pain of leaving comrades behind. He also felt bitter at the apparent lack of any protection from the Royal Air Force, not knowing that they were, in fact, flying round the clock to protect the beaches and hold up the German advance. In that remarkable act of rescue, whilst a hard core of Allied troops held up the German advance from 27th May to 5th June, 309,000 British and French personnel were picked up off the beaches at Dunkirk and brought home to England, mostly without their weapons and equipment. On their arrival at Dover they were told: "Each of you get on the train and get up to London. You'll find the RTO at Waterloo, and he'll tell you you have a couple of days to go home, and where you're to assemble to join your new units."

When Christopher reached his home in Curry Rivel, Somerset, his mother took one look at him, and said: "You look as if you need a good wash, go upstairs and have a bath!" A strange way to welcome one's son snatched from the jaws of death, but those were the days when tearful reunions were less socially acceptable. As his wife Wendy commented: "You can't say what's in your heart, you say something practical so you don't cry."

He did, however, speak a little later of what he had done. On 24th June my mother, by then with us in England, wrote to my father:

Christopher is in great form - and in his conversation I've collected bits of what he did in France. He was at Dunkirk for five days, before he evacuated - __un__loading ammunition under heavy fire - the fire was so heavy that the men were beginning to strike so he volunteered to go down into the hold and I think spent about two hours there.

Christopher had to rejoin what remained of his unit, and on his way to Aldershot, where the RASC were reforming, he stopped briefly with our Uncle Cecil and the Halliwell family in Farnham; our cousin Bill well remembers this soldier in his tattered uniform spending a night with them.

Jersey in the Front Line

So swift was the German advance that the news agencies could hardly keep up with it. Then, on 10th June Italy entered the war on the side of Germany. Winston Churchill planned to hit them hard with a raid on their northern cities. Because the targets were at the extreme range of the bombers, Churchill tried to get French agreement for them to fly from southern France. The French, fearing German retaliation, refused permission and local people near the airfields blocked the runways to prevent their use. So Jersey was chosen as a refuelling stop. I already knew by sight most of the 'planes flying, and all day on 11th June I saw black Whitley bombers with their sinister nose-heavy flight, landing and taking off at the Airport.

That night Jersey's Lieut. Governor, Major-General Harrison, complained to the Home Office about the Airport lights being turned on for the operation, and of the danger of enemy attack against which there was no defence. In an account of these events, the Airport Commandant, our friend Charles Roche, wrote:

Then the CO asked if we had airport lights. We had, I replied, but could not use them as the whole island had been in a state of blackout for months. He gave me an order to switch them on as the airport was a military one, he said, while he was in command of a vitally important air attack. So I switched on but within two or three minutes a very angry Lieut. Governor was on the phone ordering me to turn them off as I was inviting the whole island to be bombed by the Germans. I managed to get the CO to talk to him and the lights remained on.

And so, on the night of the 11th - 12th, with necessarily light loads they dropped their first bombs on the Fiat factory at Turin and the Caprioni aircraft works outside Milan. They planned to refuel again on the return journey, but because of engine trouble and bad weather, many of them came back to Jersey soon after take-off. Of the 36 bombers which set out for Italy, only eleven reached the target. However, in other respects the raid passed off uneventfully. My father must have received what we knew as a "yellow warning", to stand by in case of a raid, because in my diary I recorded: "There were lots of Whitley bombers flying about, as well as all night. We put up boards in case of an air raid, but all went well." Our blackout consisted of three-ply boards fitted in the windows. As it was midsummer, no blackout would have been needed, and the boards were put up in case of a bombing attack.

Life in Jersey at that time contained certain elements of farce. Jersey Airport was sited at the far end of our Parish of St. Peter, and John Herbert describes one particular incident:

In June, when the Evacuation commenced and regular civil aviation to the Channel Islands had ceased, the Airport Staff were told that those who wished to do so could evacuate. Charles Roche and I were ordered to remain at our posts. At this time Roche ordered that a 24 hour watch should be maintained divided into two watches of 12 hours. He also ordered me to issue a password each evening to all duty personnel, including the Commanding Officer Royal Militia Island of Jersey. The RMIJ maintained a guard (armed) at night at various vulnerable sites, including the Marconi-Adcock direction finding masts. One night I had the 1800-0600 watch when the members of the St. Peter's Honorary Police under Centenier T.G. Le Cappelain and Johnnie Vautier decided to make a security patrol of the airport. Of course they did not have the password for the night and on patrolling the Marconi-Adcock site they were promptly detained by the armed guard and marched into the Guard Room in the terminal building. I received a telephone call from the guard commander advising me that he had some trouble and could I help? I went to the Guard Room and was confronted by some very angry Hon. Police. My Jersey French was not up to 'A' Level but I got a brief inkling of what their thoughts were.

At home, unaware of the conflicts which were being fought out elsewhere in our parish, we carried on our lives as usual. However, one morning Anthony and I awoke to see a barrage balloon floating at the foot of our garden. These were used in Britain to protect important targets from air attack, the principle being that if an enemy bomber flew below them to access the target, the cable would slice through the wings of the enemy aircraft and bring it down. We knew that there were no barrage balloons in the Island so this one must have drifted across the channel, and decided to tie it up at the bottom of the garden of our house. Later in the day it disappeared. John Herbert reveals what happened:

One morning I was on the 0600-1800 watch. We still had two Air Traffic Controllers. At about 0900 hours I went up to Control to have a chat with the Duty Controller (Ivor List). At the time the Airport was covered with thick fog. We were chatting away when to our utter amazement a barrage balloon came out of the fog (trailing a cable). We alerted the Duty Crew who tried to catch the trailing cable but to no avail. Le Cappelain's cottages [near the Airport] were then supplied privately by Taff Le Cappelain, and the cable fouled the overhead supply wires and cut off the electricity. After a short while, the balloon having disappeared into the fog, I received a telephone call from a member of the public stating that the balloon had come to rest at Sandybrook with its cable tangled with the roof of a house, I believe it was 'Red Roofs'. [Actually

'Red Lodge', the home of Capt. Harry Ballantine]. We had an Aircraft Accident Recovery Vehicle with a large winch on it, so I assembled the Duty Crew and proceeded to a field adjoining the house. The St. Peter's Hon. Police were in attendance and 'my friend' Centenier Le Cappelain was on the gate. On proceeding with the lorry and crew into the field, I was stopped by the Centenier.

> *'Mr. Herbert, where do you think you are going?'*
>
> *'Centenier, I have come to lower that balloon.'*
>
> *'Oh no, you won't, you are not at the Airport now you know.'*

With some loss of dignity we returned to the Airport. Shortly afterwards the Centenier relented and we managed to lower the balloon.

On 14th June the Germans entered Paris, and the following day the *Evening Post* carried an editorial condemning "rumour mongering" which, they said, was sapping morale. At the same time notices appeared calling on able-bodied men with military experience to join the Jersey Defence Volunteers by applying to their local parish hall.

The Governor had been informed that troops were to be sent to protect the Island, which had been designated as a staging post for the British Expeditionary Force being evacuated from St. Malo, Cherbourg and Brest. A battery of Bofors guns was being sent to Jersey, one troop for the defence of the Airport and another for use either there or in St. Helier. That day troops and stores began to arrive, some on a train ferry, and a curfew from 9.00 pm to 5.00 am was put into operation. Trenches were dug for defence and telegraph poles and wires erected on Victoria Avenue to prevent the landing of troops. Bristol Blenheim fighter-bombers were flying from the Airport to reconnoitre the German advance in France.

The Lieut. Governor was asked if local sailing craft could be made available to assist in the evacuation of troops in France to waiting shipping. On the evening of 16th June the sloop HMS *Wild Swan* arrived in Jersey with eight tons of explosive and a demolition party on board, and reported to the Governor. Seven waiting potato vessels were requisitioned to sail for St. Malo and the *Wild Swan* left the same evening, arriving at St. Malo just after midnight on 17th June, dropping off the demolition party and departing. She was followed by 20 small boats from Jersey, who assisted in taking the troops to their transport. Just after midday the petrol tank depots were destroyed and, following a message that the Germans were nine miles from the town, charges were placed on the lock gates and fired. The demolition party boarded a Jersey yacht and left St. Malo just as the Germans were entering the town. For this assistance with the evacuation the St. Helier Yacht Club was awarded 'battle honours' and given the rare privilege of flying a 'defaced' red ensign, that is a flag with a naval anchor superimposed on the crossed axes of the town of St. Helier.

That day the nation's churches united in a Day of Prayer for France. The French capital had fallen, having been declared an "open city". Marshal Pétain, who had taken over the French Government, surrendered, and on 17th June the *Evening Post* carried headlines: "France ceases to fight - Germans asked for terms", adding "Britain will fight on." So the French government sued for peace, but it was some time before terms were agreed, and fighting went on for a while.

Jersey Airport, as well as providing a base for the RAF reconnaissance over France, also acted as a staging post for RAF 'planes leaving France for the UK. On 17th June a very special person stopped briefly on his way to London. In France's hour of greatest need Mr. Churchill had made the offer of a political union with Britain with joint defence and joint citizenship. This was rejected out of hand. Union with Britain would be, said Marshal Pétain, fusion with a corpse. A new government was set up in Bordeaux, and General Charles de Gaulle said he did not think he could perform any useful service there. Mr. Churchill had sent General Spears as his personal envoy to the French Prime Minister M. Reynaud. Churchill was anxious about the safety of General de Gaulle and planned to get him away. On that morning de Gaulle went to his office in Bordeaux, made a number of afternoon engagements as a blind, and accompanied General Spears to his aircraft. In his *History of the Second World War*, Churchill tells what happened next:

They shook hands and said goodbye, and as the plane began to move de Gaulle jumped in and slammed the door. The machine roared off into the air, while the French police and officials gaped. De Gaulle carried with him, in this small aeroplane, the honour of France.

The 'plane headed for Jersey.

John Herbert recalls that day in his account:

The aircraft landed here sometime between 1130 hours and midday. General de Gaulle (whose name meant nothing to me in those days) accompanied by a General Spears came to my office and requested that their aircraft be refuelled and which I arranged. They then asked if it was possible to have lunch. Because the airport restaurant was closed they agreed to have a pub lunch so I took them to the Alexandra Hotel (now St. Peter's Hotel) where the proprietor, Jack Sheppard, provided lunch.

In his autobiography de Gaulle records asking if he could have a cup of coffee. This being unavailable he was given a cup of tea and commented: *"Ça commence bien en Angleterre."* Before leaving the hotel they purchased a case of Johnnie Walker whisky. Herbert conveyed them back to the Airport and they took off about 3.00 pm. De Gaulle describes his arrival in England feeling: "Alone, without anything, like a man standing by the ocean knowing that somehow he had to cross it."

That same night General de Gaulle made his historic appeal to the French people and particularly its armed forces, calling on them to rally to the Free French cause. He ended: "France has lost a battle, she has not lost the war."

On 17th June we could hear the sound of gunfire coming from north-east of the Island. It was suggested that the Germans were bombing Cherbourg. In fact, Rommel's 7th Panzer Division were already advancing north up the Cotentin Peninsula, pursuing the British 157th Brigade which was withdrawing to the port, and the French battle-cruiser *Le Courbet*, with two torpedo-boats and three other ships, was shelling them. On the morning of the 18th the Germans were in contact with the British rearguard ten miles south of the harbour. The last ship left Cherbourg for England at 4.00 pm, when the Germans were within three miles of the port. That evening, the 7th Panzer Division entered Cherbourg. Very few British were taken prisoners.

Had we known in Jersey that the Germans were just across the water, the panic which ensued later would have broken out a good deal sooner.

That evening Mr. Churchill spoke to the nation on the radio:

The news from France is very bad. What has happened in France makes no difference to British faith and purpose. We have become the sole champion now in arms to defend the world cause. We shall fight on unconquerable until the curse of Hitler is lifted from the brows of men.

Chapter 3

Evacuation

As the situation in France was deteriorating rapidly, there was a good deal of confusion in the Island. The Bailiff, Alexander Coutanche, realising that occupation was inevitable, spoke to several key persons whose services were going to be essential. They were given the option of sending their families to the safety of the mainland or keeping them here. My father decided on the former course of action, but our next door neighbour, Beryl Fairlie, said she would prefer to remain with her husband and so she and their children Jean, Ray and Alastair, stayed in Jersey.

On Saturday, 15th June my father told us that "for the time being" we were going, with our mother, to live with our grandmother in Somerset, in the village of Curry Rivel, where Dorothea had grown up. Through the good offices of George Le Cocq, the Railways' agent at No. 9 Bond Street, he obtained tickets for us all on the evening sailing on 18th June. We were told we could take a few of our possessions, in addition to our clothes which were packed into trunks. I went round with a notebook making a list, which I submitted to my parents. The following day Richard celebrated his third birthday. And on Tuesday, 18th June (our parents' thirteenth wedding anniversary), as the evening sun was beginning to go down behind us, and shining on the dark clouds to the east above Fort Regent, my father drove us all down to St. Helier Harbour. At Bel Royal a solitary member of the Jersey Defence Volunteers leant on the sea wall, looking out to sea. At the far end of Victoria Avenue huge poles were being erected along the road with wires stretched across to prevent the landing of troops from the air.

At the Harbour we met two other children, the daughters of Lt. Col. Henry Vatcher, Commanding Officer of the Jersey Militia, who were coming to live with us for the time being. We reached the gangway, our father kissed us "good bye" and we climbed aboard, finding places behind the aft funnel which kept us warm! Our boat was the *Hantonia* built in 1925. She had been the last ship to leave St. Malo on 16th June, sailing direct to Southampton with 700 passengers, doubtless returning direct to Jersey the following day.

But how safe were we? No one spoke of our anxieties, for all this could have been a normal peace time sailing to England. But this was not peace time. In these early years of the war, many ships had already been lost to mines and aerial attack. In his *History of the Second World War* Churchill tells how Hitler had hinted darkly about a "secret weapon" to which there was no counter measure. One night an Admiral had come to see him in great anxiety, as six ships had been inexplicably sunk in the approaches to the Thames. By a stroke of luck later that month a German aircraft was seen to drop a large object attached to a parachute into the sea off Shoeburyness, overlooking the fact that the river was tidal at this point. The mine was recovered and taken to Portsmouth for examination. It was a magnetic mine which lay on the seabed and would be exploded by the magnetic field of any ship passing over it. A method of demagnetising ships was then devised by girdling them with an electric cable, called "degaussing". Some 4,000 British ships needed equipping with degaussing girdles. I was very glad to notice that the *Hantonia* was marked with yellow crosses round her hull above an enormous cable which went completely round the ship – the degaussing girdle; and in the stern she was equipped with an anti-aircraft gun. So we were as well protected as we could be.

In addition to our 303 passengers, we carried all the bonds and securities from the Jersey banks.

It was feared that if the Germans got their hands on them, they could sell them in the money markets on the Continent, and America and the British Government would be powerless to intervene. Bank officials had worked night and day to complete the documentation and pack the bonds and share certificates into some 100 sacks. At 5.00 pm, as the *Hantonia* left, the train ferry *Hampton* was anchored in St. Aubin's Bay and Bofors light anti-aircraft guns were being landed in the Old Harbour (the only ramp available) for the defence of the Airport.

It was quite a cold night, but we all slept well on deck close to our lifejackets which were stacked nearby in case of need. At 4.00 am we woke to a glorious sunrise, and a few hours later were safely cruising up Southampton Water, passing a small fleet of Belgian passenger ships which had escaped to safety before the Germans' arrival.

Not surprisingly, my father was acutely anxious about our safety. On our arrival my mother had sent a telegram. On 19th June he wrote: "Darling, I've been completely on edge waiting for your wire which didn't arrive until about 12.30. Thank God you're all safe. Now I could face Hitler himself. You got out just in time, believe me."

The Royal Militia Island of Jersey had been mobilised at the outbreak of war and was quartered in Fort Regent. The Commanding Officer, Lt. Col. Vatcher, having seen his children off with us to England, that night received orders for demilitarisation. He informed the Lieut. Governor who announced this to the States. He requested permission to disband his force, as it was raised solely for island defence. The men then volunteered for service in the British Army.

Tension and Panic

At the outbreak of war my parents had laid in extra stocks of food; two large earthenware jars, about four feet high, were filled with salted beans, and another with eggs conserved in waterglass. In the event they could not have lasted very long, but they must have come in useful during the years of occupation. My father also took the precaution of burying all the family silver in the garden; actually there was no looting of this kind and the Germans were to prove very correct in their attitude to the possessions of the civilian population.

For the next few days my parents wrote to each other daily. My father's letters vividly reflect the atmosphere of tension and uncertainty of island life at the time, and each one is written as if it could have been the last. Despite the desperate military situation, the RAF, who were to be the saviours of Britain in a few weeks' time were, he reported, very positive about their role over the Islands.

On 19th June he wrote:

Yesterday there was a Heinkel and a Messerschmitt playing about. Our fighters went up and drove them off. One of them was bitterly disappointed: he'd just got back from France and had 7 to his credit and was hoping to make it even numbers. Their spirit is marvellous and all they talk about is how soon they can up and at them.

I don't know what the policy is to be here, but all our people are out of Northern France. That is no secret now.

Colonel Vatcher dropped in with his wife. My father wrote:

Beryl and Henry came. He looked desperately tired until he'd had a drink. We all felt better after that, marvellous effect it has. I'm taking some of my sherry down to the hospital in case I have to do long hours. Miss Millar [the Matron] will be horrified but I cannot help that. I'm burying the silver in the garden.

At that time he was even thinking of joining her in England: "Don't worry about me, I'm alright and <u>very</u> cheerful now. I'll try to slip out if there is general evacuation and if I haven't anything useful to do here, but I <u>must</u> await orders. Give the children my love and a little bit more for yourself."

The same day he wrote again, a letter containing two substantial cheques. As the Post Office could not guarantee any mail, he rushed to the Airport, found an acquaintance there, Mrs. Willis, wife of a former Governor, and gave it to her to post. He was fortunate, because the last 'plane left the following day.

He wrote:

Dearest, I hope that by now you have recovered from your nightmare and have had a good night's rest.

Tension here has been terrific. We woke up this morning expecting to be bombed to blazes any time. Then came the news that the island was to be demilitarised and declared open. As quickly as they have appeared, all the guns vanished. Lorries, armoured cars hurtled down the front all afternoon, embarking stores and ammunition. I never realised they had so many, they must have landed hundreds. The RAF vanished and now all is quiet, except in the Town where panic reigns.

There is to be a sort of voluntary evacuation of women and children and men of military age, all of whom have to register at the Town Hall before 10-0 tomorrow. I have never seen such a pitiful exhibition of panic.

During the campaign in France and the Low Countries the work of the Allied troops had been seriously hampered by the huge numbers of panicking refugees, fleeing from the advancing Germans, who clogged the roads. There was clearly a similar panic in Jersey, but the different geography and the official provision of transport meant that there were no such problems. The British government learnt a lesson here, and in a leaflet, which was delivered to our household later in June and entitled 'If the Invader comes', we were firmly told to remain at home in the event of invasion.

On Thursday 20th my father wrote, listing the doctors who had already left and wondering how many would remain. The next day he added:

A marvellous crowd of boats have just anchored in the Bay - a real Harry Tate's Navy - all sizes and shapes. I suppose they are what was left over after Dunkirk. Those poor fools are packed like sardines and God help them if a gale springs up. One thing is certain: people who have run away from their jobs will get no consideration after this war. I thought of many things I wanted to say to you last night, but now they've all gone out of my mind. Don't worry about me. I'm quite alright and very cheerful. I shall have plenty to occupy my mind - and hands, and I hope to finish my wall before the war is over.

I shall be thinking about you all, always. The only thing that matters is for us to beat these devils. I'll try to get another letter off tomorrow.

All my love dearest and kiss the children for me.

About this time a member of the staff of the *Evening Post*, Leslie Sinel, started keeping a diary, and this, his *Occupation Diary*, became a wonderful source of news of the events of those five years. Because of his position and the clever use he made of it, he was able to record a host of significant episodes, many of which were not fully interpreted until the war was over.

On 20th June Sinel recorded:

The evacuation proceeds. The piers are crowded with people, and many boats, including colliers, leave filled to capacity, among the troops being the Militia of 11 officers and 193 other ranks, for the Isle of Wight.

On the morning of 21st June the Bailiff was sworn in as Civil Governor and the Lieut. Governor departed. The *Evening Post*, under a bold heading, "EVACUATION", reported that shipping facilities were being provided for immediate voluntary evacuation to the UK of women and children. Enormous queues formed at the Town Hall stretching some ¾ mile, the whole length of the Parade and into Gloucester Street, to obtain tickets for the boats.

On 22nd June my father wrote:

There is still no sign of Hitler, so this may get away… I could fill a book with stories of the Jersey panic, but it's too awful and I'll say no more about it… An amusing thing happened yesterday. Who should ring the bell at 9.30 am but Mr. Le Quesne the entomologist. He had come back from Oxford as there wasn't much doing and had taken two Dark Green Fritillaries [rare butterflies]. He was far more excited about these than the presence of the Germans in St. Malo - which is after all the right spirit.

Chapter 4
The General Hospital Reorganises

At the Jersey General Hospital, as the evacuation proceeded, there was also a measure of panic. My father wrote:

I went to Hospital and found Miss Millar [the Matron] packing her things. I tried to reason with her, but she was completely hysterical, so I gathered all the nurses who were standing round in shoals like sheep and gave them a damned good row. I think I managed to put some sense into their heads, but I think they are all afraid of being raped by the Germans. Talking about that, one Jerseyman told me he was evacuating his daughter aged 16 for the same reason. I wanted to say that raping was probably inevitable for her wherever she was, and that nationality didn't seem to be important… I don't know how many people will be left, but I must stay: if you had seen the panic you would understand.

O'Connor was seeing his family off when the news came through, when he stepped on to the boat without a ticket, without his things, and left his car on the quay! Lewis flew off in an Army plane and there are rumours about other people going. [Dr. John Lewis later returned and was a staunch member of the medical team]. I cannot leave these people helpless. The Dispensary [a small cottage hospital] nurses left in a body to register: I suppose they'll all go. We shall probably have to shut it down and form a skeleton Nursing Service at the Hospital, but at the moment it is chaos - nobody in charge, nobody to give advice. So I've had to take some sort of charge and try to produce order. By tomorrow the atmosphere may be better.

Now about money. I've raised quite a lot and it will reach you by devious ways, so I think you will be able to carry on until this war is over, which I do not think will be long. Germany has got to force a win by the autumn and I'm sure that sea-power plus our air force will beat them. In the meantime I have to look forward to separation from you all without news: that is the worst thing about it - no news. But it won't last long.

Thursday (June 20th). The panic continues. I wouldn't have believed it possible. I've read about mass hysteria and had always been rather sceptical about it. But here it is, and it's extraordinarily interesting.

McKinstry [Medical Officer of Health], Blampied [General Practitioner] and I have been trying to get authority to organise the Medical Services, and then we shall know where we are. I've evacuated the Dispensary to the General and all the nurses except Matron are already out.

Millbrook exchange rang me up this morning and said they were putting no more calls through, as they were all clearing out. I argued with the girl and tried to reduce her to sanity. The service has now been resumed so I suppose somebody has organised it… I hope Hitler doesn't know about all this: it would certainly cheer him up. I did one op at the Hospital this morning to try to give them something to think about.

Keep cheerful and think of the marvellous holiday we are going to have when this show is over. Madeira would be rather nice. I'm rather off the French at the moment. All my love, dearest to you all. Arthur.

The scene at the Hospital that day is well described by an Irish nurse, Mauyen Keane, in her book, *Hello, Is It All Over?* The Bailiff had announced that, following the fall of Paris, the invasion of Jersey might be only a matter of days:

Loudspeakers blared out, advising people to remain calm, that free passage to the mainland would be available as long as possible. Inside the hospital, doctors, nurses and porters were rushing here and there. All of Matron's staff seemed to be queuing up outside her office to pick up their diplomas or references. Others went straight over to the hotel to pack, not even bothering to do that. I remember entering the office and seeing Matron's face as she signed papers for her staff, pausing every now and then as she wrote to look up with pleading eyes, desperately hoping that at least some of us would stay.

Mauyen Keane describes my father's "damned good row" from her perspective:

The familiar voice of our lecturer, Mr. Halliwell, was heard over the loudspeaker. He was calling all the nurses to the committee room which also acted as a lecture room. Matron's pen dropped from her hand with relief and we all followed her to hear what Mr. Halliwell had to say. We found him standing beside the skeleton, his usual position. How wonderful it would be, I thought, if this were just another ordinary day. The sun shone on his troubled face and his proud Englishman's voice began to tremble as he addressed us:

'Nurses, I have decided to send my wife and children to the mainland and I advise those of you who have ties there to leave. I know you will depart with the dignity befitting your profession. This is a very grave time for all of us and we have no way of knowing how long we may be under German rule. Prisoners we will be, of course, but naturally those of you who volunteer to stay will be most welcome. Let me assure you that you will be needed.'

Silently we filed out of the room as though we had been given tranquillizers.

Mary Le Sueur (then Sister Mary Jouny) recalls how most of the Irish nurses went down to the harbour, hoping to leave. But there was no boat and they had to stay. Mary said to them: "You wouldn't have been able to live with yourselves if you had all left us." Keane and her colleagues were glad that they had not all succeeded in leaving. She continues:

We went straight on to all the wards and the welcome we received made us very happy in our professions as nurses. As we rushed from ward to ward we were welcomed by a grateful Mr. Halliwell and the medical officer (Dr. Averell Darling) both of whom were unable to conceal their relief and delight.

At the outbreak of war Jersey had seen the arrival of two newly qualified doctors, Dr. Henderson from Trinity College, Dublin, and Dr. Darling from Queen's University, Belfast.

Dr. Darling, who was still alive and resident in our parish when this book was being prepared, kindly wrote a full account of his time at the Hospital as a colleague of my father:

I arrived on Thursday 7th September and was soon in the Jersey General Hospital. I was granted a few minutes for breakfast and was then handed a white coat and almost pushed into casualty by Dr. Henderson, who was also newly qualified from Trinity College, Dublin. I had only been at work for a short time when Mr. Halliwell broke off his round to welcome me to my first full time post. His welcome was so warm and as kindly as one could wish and this attitude to his juniors never changed. There must have been many times when we, raw recruits as we were, must have fallen short of his expectations but he remained patient and understanding and never blew his top. We were never afraid of him but always respected him and liked him. We quickly realised what an expert surgeon he was. He worked to the highest standards and naturally expected the same from us. He was that ideal combination, a thinking physician who possessed a first class pair of hands and surgical technique. He was always open to new advances and ready to listen to suggestions and ideas from any quarter - especially if they came from St. Thomas's, his own teaching hospital. We enjoyed working with him and felt privileged to work under him and to be taught by him.

Darling described his enthusiasm for his work. One day, when opening up a patient for an operation, he looked at Darling and exclaimed delightedly: "We've got this one!"

It was once unkindly said of St. Thomas's, "You can always tell a Thomas's man, but you can never tell him anything!" Clearly this was not Averell Darling's view. To him, 'ACH' (as he was generally known) was "the nucleus around which all the constituent parts of the 'cell' took their place, each playing its part to form the whole."

Darling explained that "Sister Tutor (Miss Bissell) with the help of other senior nurses kept the nursing school in business, and kept Mr. Halliwell busy as lecturer." Former nurse Betty Thurban (née Le Corre) remembers these lectures:

There was a teaching room next to matron's office. Mr. Halliwell used to do lots of teaching on the wards, and then give his lectures from 5.00 pm till 6.00 pm. He was very good at this. He was a most wonderful man, and there is no doubt that he enthused you with the subjects of his lectures. You listened to him because of who he was, and you came to share his enthusiasm. He was a delightful man but I don't think people would happily cross him. There was never any doubt when he wasn't pleased.

Darling remembered his kindness to his colleagues:

He was kindness itself. When I did something wrong, he never once corrected me by saying I should not have done something, he merely used to show me in an oblique way what he would have done had he been there. He was a physician first and foremost, and he took such an interest in the whole person. He was also a perfect surgeon, and in a way that was the problem. I find it very difficult to say anything negative, he was so patient and gentle and so keen on his work. But it has to be said, shy man that he was, he was too reserved with his patients. He was also a man of a great sense of humour. One day I told him of a patient who had been admitted with a hernia. I said he was quite old, and he asked me how old. I said he was in his middle forties. ACH [who was 44 at the time] went on for quite a long time, saying: 'Not old, Darling, not old, Darling!'

My father had spoken to the two Resident Medical Officers and asked that one of them should stay. Dr. Darling's colleague, Dr. Henderson, felt it his duty to return to the mainland and join up. Darling commented: "My convictions were different and I felt I should stay. I discussed the position with Mr. Halliwell and much to my surprise he told me that if I was prepared to stay he would be in favour. I stayed and never for one moment regretted doing so."

Fortunately, Dr. Henderson's place was taken by a medical student from St. Bartholomew's Hospital who had returned to visit his parents in Jersey. They had evacuated and he was left stranded. Raymond Osmont had completed the first two years of his studies but this time had not been a great success, and he had not been involved in the clinical side. However, Averell Darling and ACH had faith in his abilities, and took him under their wing.

In a paper written for the Société Jersiaise Dr. Osmont paid tribute to Darling's training of him, and his dedication:

For the first six months he had the very unenviable task of trying to instill in me the principles and practice of clinical medicine. However he withstood such a task with equanimity and an ever present dry sense of humour.

He remained as the only resident doctor. In the ensuing five years he devoted all his knowledge, skill and energy for 24 hours of every day in the constant care of all those innumerable patients who were seen and treated by him in the so-called normal course of his duties.

It is said that he and ACH turned him into an excellent surgical assistant. He completed his studies after the war and was later awarded the MBE.

Raymond Osmont mentioned that Dr. John Hanna was in charge of the medical wards, and Mr. Arnold Ferguson was surgeon in charge of both the Eye, and Ear, Nose and Throat Departments. Doctors Warrington and Blampied, both GPs, were anaesthetists, and Dr. Wood was radiologist for a short time.

Dentistry was in the hands of Mr. Joe Price, named the "Mad Hatter". Dr. Osmont explained:

The dental clinic was presided over by Mr. Joe Price, presided over being the right description, as the dental department throughout these years was the most popular rendezvous for senior medical staff, for the very good reason that Joe Price had an inexhaustible supply of pre-war Mazawattee tea and so these 'Mad Hatter's Tea Parties' were able to continue throughout the five years.

Mary Le Sueur remembers these parties well: "They used to have these meetings every Monday morning, I don't know what for, and talk at great length. I was now a sister, so I felt able to approach Mr. Halliwell and I said to him 'What do you talk about all the time?' He looked at me and smiled, 'We talk about lots of things, especially the sisters!'"

Dr. Darling also explained that whilst Matron, Miss Millar, was left with a very depleted nursing staff, many senior nursing sisters remained and Matron regrouped her forces around these sisters. Sister Norwood took over the male wards, Sister Litt stayed as theatre sister, and Mrs. Blackburn was sister in charge of the Maternity Ward. Sister Davey continued as home sister and Sister Mary Jouny took care of Out Patients and Casualty. A recruitment campaign was instituted in the schools to encourage girls of school leaving age to take up nursing as a career. This provided the Hospital with a very ready supply of nurses throughout the Occupation years.

At the outbreak of war Elise Floyd, whose father was Vicar of St. James's Church, was training as a physiotherapist. At my father's suggestion, in January, 1940 she had returned to London to complete her training and take her examinations. However, when the British Expeditionary Force was driven out of France at Dunkirk and the fall of France became a possibility she was quickly brought home. Her exam results had arrived just before the Germans, and so Jersey had a newly trained physiotherapist ready to join the team. At this time, Miss Lowry, who was in charge of both the Physiotherapy and X-Ray Departments, decided to give up the Physiotherapy and concentrate on X-Ray. My father had taken a great deal of interest in Elise's career, perhaps because my mother had trained as a physiotherapist at St. Thomas's where she had done pioneering work, and he appointed her head of the department. He had a clinic there every week and seemed to derive strength from the more relaxed, peaceful and informal atmosphere that prevailed there.

Miss Lowry now headed up the X-Ray Department. With the arrival of the Germans there were problems concerning regular supplies of X-ray film. Fortunately, arrangements were made with the German authorities for this to be obtained from Holland, and as their equipment was also made in Holland, by Phillips, the film and equipment matched perfectly. The department was also responsible for dental X-rays of the German military, who did not have the necessary equipment, but provided their own film. In those early days Miss Lowry was forced to make her position clear to the Germans. A German officer came and greeted her with "Heil Hitler!" She retorted: "Don't you Heil Hitler me!" and so he replied: "Good Morning Madame." Miss Lowry feared repercussions, but nothing more was said.

Later on Lorna Mackintosh (now du Pré) joined the department and remembers the effect of the special clamp they used to keep the head steady. The soldiers were not accustomed to this, and when it was attached, used at first to leap out of the chair fearing they were about to be electrocuted. With reassurance they settled down. On one occasion a German came in for attention and Lorna, not knowing he understood her, said: "He'll have to wait." He replied in perfect English, "That will be quite all right."

Averell Darling completes the medical line-up:

Our medical officer of health, Dr. R.N.M. McKinstry, from Banbridge, Co. Down also stayed. He was a very clever doctor and being trained in the old ways of medical officers of health, he was an excellent microbiologist who specialised in the prevention and control of the infectious diseases. He ran Overdale Hospital [an isolation hospital] and was in charge of the laboratory at the General Hospital. In addition to the routine microbiology he, with his technical laboratory assistant provided a really good blood transfusion service. Many hundreds of pints of cross-matched blood would be supplied during the Occupation years and the service never failed to meet the demands. Our deputy chief engineer Herbert Dallain stepped into the chief's post and his department never let us down. Snowdon Amy our pharmacist, stayed and worked wonders. One after another, the vacancies were filled and we were happily and enthusiastically in business.

My father lists the posts held, though there were some changes from time to time:

Matron: Miss Millar (resigned owing to ill health April, 1941)

Assistant Matron: Miss Carter (appointed Matron 23rd April 1941)

Home Sister: Miss Davey

Administrative Sister: Miss Clegg (died in 1944)

Out Patients Sister: Miss Litt

Male Ward: Miss Barnett (later Mrs. Quénault)

Female Ward: Miss Norwood who afterwards took charge of Les Vaux TB sanatorium

Ward for chronic sick: Miss Renouard

Medical and Surgical Staff

Surgeon: A.C. Halliwell FRCS

Physician: Dr. Hanna

Radiologist: Dr. Warrington   Radiographer: Miss Lowry

Eye, Ear, Nose & Throat Surgeon: Mr. Ferguson (died during the war)

Anaesthetist: Dr. Blampied

Dental Surgeon: Mr. Price

Resident Medical Officer: Dr. Darling

Unqualified R.M.O.: Mr. Osmont, later Dr. Osmont

During these years there were also seventeen General Practitioners in active practice and in addition to the usual difficulties, such as limited supplies of drugs and dressings they, like many others, had also to resort to bicycles with solid tyres. One GP, Dr. Florence Sexton, even rode to her patients on horseback.

The Halliwell family in the late 1930s.
(L to R) My mother Dorothea, Anthony, myself, Daphne, my father Arthur ('ACH') and Richard.

'Le Clos du Chemin'.

My father relaxing in his garden just before the evacuation. Although barely visible, the newspaper's front page maps out the German advance.

ACH at the beginning of the Occupation. Compare this with his appearance in 1945 when the years of strain had taken their toll.

Old cannon in People's Park with "Calling Out" notices for HM Army and Air Force, 23rd September 1939. *Jersey Evening Post*

The "Sandbag Brigade" at Springfield, 23rd September 1939. *Jersey Evening Post*

The runaway barrage balloon that caused so much trouble in the Parish of St. Peter in 1940.
Jersey Evening Post

Anti-invasion measures: stretching wires over Victoria Avenue to prevent German aircraft from landing, June, 1940. *Jersey Evening Post*

Despite the rapid German advance, potatoes are still exported: lorries queue at St. Helier Harbour in June, 1940, oblivious to the fact that, to German aerial reconnaissance, they resemble ammunition trucks. Days later the Harbour will be bombed… *Jersey Evening Post*

Queueing at the Town Hall to register for evacuation, June, 1940. *Jersey Evening Post*

(Above and below) Evacuation scenes at the Weighbridge, June, 1940. *Jersey Evening Post*

Chapter 5
Final Days of Freedom

At Jersey Airport, John Herbert was trying to cope with desperate people trying to get seats on the few 'planes available. He recalled that he was offered "houses, cars, money" if he would but favour this person or that. It was reported that half the population had registered for evacuation. Panic took over, with properties being abandoned or sold to neighbours for as little as £5, and the Animals' Shelter appealed to the public to bring in to them any abandoned animals they should find; reporting that 2,200 dogs and 3,000 cats had been destroyed in the last few days. The Island was saddened by the suicide by gassing of our neighbour, the popular Danish Vice-Consul, Mr. A.E.P. Andersen, who had seen his wife and son off at the Harbour, promising to join them later. Nearly 10,000 people left the Island, and some 41,000 remained. The last 'plane left on 20th June.

The Germans now occupied the French mainland, and the German Admiral Commanding France discussed with the operations staff of *Luftflotte 3* plans for taking the Channel Islands. Reconnaissance by *2 Aufkl. Gruppe 123* was ordered, but was done from such a height that the Germans had great difficulty in interpreting the photographs. The reports suggested there were defence installations near the Harbour and some forts "surrounded by woodlands". Nothing was known of their state nor even if they were manned. In fact, queues of potato lorries and civilian transports were mistaken for legitimate military targets. Lengthy discussions took place about what to do. One thing was clear: there must be no failure to mar the conclusion of such a successful campaign.

In Jersey the next few days were a strange mixture of normality and apprehension, waiting for the inevitable. By 21st June the immediate panic had subsided and the paper reported that businesses were reopening. In a notice in the press the Dean, Matthew Le Marinel, reported that all services would be held as normal in the Island churches on the coming Sunday. He added: "It is those whose faith is stayed in God who are level headed, clear visioned and sober minded and who can act with courage, wisdom, confidence, endurance and fortitude." He is remembered as a priest who was at the altar of his church every day for the next five years trying to put this into practice.

Shortly before the outbreak of war, Mr. Newbery and Mrs. Lock, with her daughter Audrey, had come to Jersey seeking work. Initially, Mr. Newbery was engaged as gardener at 'Le Clos du Chemin', and after the evacuation they all moved into the house, Mrs. Lock (generally known as 'Mrs. Newbery'), being employed as housekeeper. The couple were to be a great source of support to my father in the difficult times that lay ahead.

On 23rd June my father wrote his last letter to me:

'I shouldn't think you got much sleep - knowing you - but I expect Woodey [my brother] was doggo as usual… You were heavily escorted as you carried all the bonds and securities from the Jersey banks. That was rather important because if the Germans had captured them they would be able to sell them in neutral countries for oil and other things they want.

Jersey has settled down after the evacuation. About 25,000 people registered to go, but only 9,000 odd actually left.

We have had a number of refugees from France, soldiers and sailors, French, Poles, Czechs. A few English are still drifting back, chiefly wounded, but there have been more during the last 24 hours.

We are quite happy here and very busy. Audrey (Mrs. Newbery's girl) who is just about 12 - 13 has adopted 'Twink' [our dog], in spite of the fact that he doesn't get his daily ration of meat. I am very disappointed I missed seeing our warships shelling the Germans advancing on St. Malo [Cherbourg] during the evacuation. I think it was the day before you left and lots of people saw it from the north of the Island.

Give my love to everybody and tell Woodey I'll write to him tomorrow.

On 26th June my father heard the Germans flying high over the Island, in fact taking reconnaissance photographs. He wrote to my mother:

There seems to be quite a lot of aerial activity here this evening. I don't know whose they are, but the noise has been fairly constant for about a couple of hours. They must be very high up.

There was a low-level reconnaissance the following day, and ACH wrote:

June 27. A boat came in today bringing food and newspapers. I expect there was a mail, but nothing has turned up so far.

Some planes flew low over the town today and everyone saw crosses on them… With any luck we may be able to see an air battle, though I hope it will be over the sea and not over our garden… I expect this cargo boat will go out this evening. This harbour isn't very healthy for shipping. All my love to you dearest and keep cheerful.

This was the last letter which got through.

The next day the harbour and town were bombed and four days later the Germans landed.

Dr. Darling describes what happened:

On Thursday 28th June the Luftwaffe paid us a visit. I watched three Heinkel bombers fly over the harbour area. As I watched I saw the first bombs begin to fall and I took off for casualty, getting there just before the ambulance brought in the first victim of the raid. From his home on high ground, some miles from the hospital, Mr Halliwell was also watching the Heinkels. He too saw the bombs begin their fall, and he took off, reaching the hospital in record time. He worked incessantly in the theatre until the small hours of the morning, assisted by some General Practitioners.

Despite their best endeavours, ten persons died. Three days later the bombers returned, with small parachutes bearing demands for surrender.

Chapter 6
Occupied

The occupation of the Channel Islands was different to that of other European nations. Firstly, this was British territory, and from this flowed two significant factors, one positive, the other negative. On the positive side was the fact that the German authorities, perhaps recognising their racial kinship with the British, were concerned to show that they could behave in a disciplined and humane manner. On the negative side was Hitler's immense pride in his piece of British territory. In progressive instructions, he ordered the construction of defences far stronger than any others on his 'Atlantic Wall' and called by some of his officers *"Inselwahn"* or "Island madness." Secondly, because of the small size of the Islands, occupiers and occupied lived cheek by jowl in a way that was not paralleled elsewhere. This led to bouts of paranoia on the part of the Germans concerning security which sometimes occasioned harsh punishments for comparatively trivial offences. It also meant that different and conflicting attitudes developed amongst the Islanders concerning the correct attitude to adopt to the occupier. The burning question which everyone faced was: "What exactly constitutes collaboration?" Schoolchildren dared not chat to soldiers on the beach, young boys dared not let them join in their games of football, professional people, clergy and doctors dared not be seen in the company of their German opposite numbers; all for fear they should be called "collaborators".

In the early days occupier and occupied got on reasonably well and the bitter experience of occupations elsewhere in Europe seemed not to be repeated. But, in later years, as the *Reich* tightened its grip, radios were banned, and deportations ordered. Amongst the Germans, a gulf widened between the relatively benign Anglophile administrators and the increasingly hardline military. The military themselves were also divided between the professional soldiers who had a strong sense of honour and duty and the party members whose fanaticism ruled their heads. Bailiff Coutanche came to realise that in dealing with the Germans he was in fact dealing with a nation which possessed distinct entities. Though they ostensibly shared a common war aim, they did not always agree about the means whereby this aim was to be achieved. In the course of time the two began to separate out, and in the end, some opposition groups emerged. Some of the military steadfastly refused to compromise their principles by joining the party, never giving the Nazi salute; others joined the better to undermine the regime.

The Commander-in-Chief took up residence in Government House, which had been left in good order by the departing Governor, and where the Irish butler, who had been left in charge by the outgoing Governor, remained to serve the incoming Commandant! He was a Silesian nobleman of the old school, Graf von Schmettow. For his offices he took over the house in St. Saviour's Road where we had lived from our birth until our move to St. Peter in 1935. By then it was called 'Monaco', in our time it was 1 Caesarea Place. But we always called it 'The Old House'. Outside the house a huge banner was stretched across the road, proclaiming: *"BEFEHLSHABER DER BRITISCHEN KANALINSELN"* ("Commander-in-Chief of the British Channel Islands").

Von Schmettow had been gassed in the First World War and he was sent to Jersey because it was believed the climate would be good for his health. He was held in very high regard by the military and it was well known that any soldier guilty of a misdemeanour would be immediately shipped out of the Island. He also came to be well respected by the island population.

In his memoirs Coutanche tells of their relationship, describing him as:

A typical soldier [who] reminded me very much of the British generals with whom I had had so long to deal, in the persons of the Lieut-Governors of Jersey. He was smart, well dressed and dignified, and the kind of man with whom one would be instinctively careful not to take any liberties. He was the head of a very ancient Silesian family, with long military traditions. Schmettow and I reached an early agreement … that we were enemies and that there must be no sort of social intercourse between us. Within those limits, however, we could still behave like gentlemen and that was what we tried to do… I knew, and he knew that I knew, that he was being spied on.

When I used to go down and see him at his headquarters [by this time at the Hotel Metropole] … we used to sit in his large office which had been the drawing room when it was a private house, and had a large balcony leading off it. Here was posted a sentry who would periodically march up and down the balcony, guarding the General. These sentries were of course continually being changed and Schmettow was suspicious of some of them. He consequently treated them all as spies. In our conversations, when the sentry approached, he used to hold up his finger to me in order that I might say nothing while the sentry was passing. It was a strange thing that here was the Commander-in-Chief, surrounded by officers and aides, being spied on by members of the Nazi party amongst the troops.

It has sometimes been claimed that the Bailiff and his colleagues were too compliant with the occupiers, but they were more vulnerable than many people realised. Dr. Peter Falla, who lived throughout the period, believes:

If the civil administration had refused to co-operate, the Germans would have taken over. There is no doubt in my mind that if there had come a point in which the German administration were to say to the Jersey authorities 'The situation is impossible' someone would have been sent from the French mainland to sort things out.

There is some evidence to suggest that the local administration were anxious to keep everything on an even keel because of the danger of the feared Nazi *SS (Schutzstaffel)* being sent over to maintain order. Beginning as a small unit for the personal defence of the *Führer*, they developed into Hitler's private army and were responsible for vast numbers of atrocities throughout Europe. Dr. John Lewis describes his first encounter with the occupiers:

Late that afternoon, I was astonished - I don't know exactly why, because we were all expecting it - to see a young German soldier riding fairly slowly towards the town on a small collapsible motor bike. He was followed, about fifty yards behind, by two more similarly mounted - all very young, grim faced, but at the same time, incongruously self-conscious. I stopped the car to have a good look and a passer-by told me that they had landed by parachute at the airport. They brought their machines with them, and assembled them on the ground… They were followed soon after by several bodies of infantry who had landed in troop carriers and who marched to St. Helier in absolute silence. This was quite unlike their subsequent behaviour when they sang hearty patriotic songs in praise of the Reich.

An amusing incident took place when the Germans decided to visit the local prison.

The Government Secretary, Colonel Hulton, was John Lewis's father-in-law, and in *A Doctor's Occupation*, Lewis describes what happened:

Within a few days of the Germans' arrival Colonel Hulton received a note from a high-ranking official saying: 'Colonel M. presents his compliments to Colonel Hulton, and wishes to inspect the island prison. Colonel Hulton will meet him there tomorrow, Tuesday, at 8.30 am'. … He was not a man to be bullied easily and, had the note been a little less peremptory, would have answered differently, for his manners were impeccable. Instead his reply was:

'Colonel H.H. Hulton, DSO MC, presents his compliments to Colonel M. and notes that he wishes to inspect the local prison on Tuesday next at 8.30 am. Unfortunately Colonel Hulton is in the habit of breakfasting at that hour, but will be pleased to meet Colonel M. at 9.30 am.'

On Tuesday Colonel M. arrived at the appointed hour. Lewis continues:

Colonel Hulton exuded charm. He ceremoniously presented Captain Foster, then prison governor, to Colonel M. and with the Colonel's ADC and the Head Warder they started their tour. As the short term prisoners had all been released at the start of the Occupation the prison was practically empty and their visit was soon over. On their return to the main hall, the German, suspicious of the shortness of the tour, said, 'Now I will inspect the political prisoners.' Colonel Hulton's answer to that was,

'I am pleased to tell you that we have no such things and never have had.'

The German, by now getting short of patience, struck the table smartly with his cane and rapped out: 'Enough of this nonsense! I wish to see them this instant.' Patiently, Colonel Hulton, savouring every moment of the encounter, and speaking very slowly and distinctly, as if to someone of rather feeble mind, said: 'In a free country, we do not have such things as political prisoners.'

The German, fighting annoyance with disbelief, was silent for an appreciable time, then said wonderingly: 'Mein Gott, what a nation.'

On another occasion an officer was visiting the Mental Hospital, subsequently renamed St. Saviour's Hospital. On being shown the patients he commented, with chilling brevity: "We have other ways of dealing with such people."

Even allowing for a possible mistranslation of the German word *behandeln*, (meaning "to treat") the meaning is clear. Later, towards the end of the war, an unsuccessful attempt was made to deport the patients to Germany, clearly for extermination.

At 'Le Clos du Chemin', Audrey Lock was also getting used to seeing the Germans around:

I can remember the day the first Germans came. My mother and I were out on our bicycles, going towards St. Peter's airport. I don't know what I imagined they were going to be; and suddenly these two men came walking along, with green uniforms, they just looked like normal soldiers really. And then we went into the town, they were all over the place. It was horrible.

Lewis continues with the story:

Every day we saw fresh batches of Germans wandering through the town and looking with amazement at the articles displayed in shop windows. Whatever the military strength of the Reich, it was evident that its people were kept very short of consumer goods. Very soon, although it was verboten they began buying in increasing quantities and a little later on I realised that anything one needed for the bleak days ahead must be snapped up very quickly.

Lewis was at pains to point out that the Germans' broad policy was to preserve, as far as their own interests allowed, the basic individual liberty and welfare of the island community:

Shortage of supplies and the consequent deprivation we suffered were by no means entirely their fault, but rather of that strip of sea which separated us from the French mainland. The considerable harassment, especially towards the end, by our own RAF naturally increased their difficulties and hence ours. It is true that the occupying forces always had bigger rations, more fuel, more light and more privileges, but they were the top dogs, temporarily at least; in similar circumstances, I suspect that our own army would have been as tough or tougher. As a general rule, the private soldier behaved admirably and the few ugly scenes which took place, occurred mainly when the Germans were drunk, which was seldom. Cases of rape, for instance, could be counted on the fingers of one hand.

There was, too, a measure of German respect for British tradition which sometimes caused surprise. The organisers of a boxing match in St. Helier asked special permission for the National Anthem to be played. The Commandant consented, providing the doors remained closed. At the end, the organisers noticed a German officer who had come to see the match, and doubtless to see that all was in order. They began to play the National Anthem. To their surprise, the German officer stood and came to the salute.

My father recalled how the Germans occupying one of the neighbouring houses used to salute him as he drove by. He could not understand this and hazarded the guess that they mistook his blue grey flannel suit for the uniform of a German *Luftwaffe* officer. Such was the atmosphere of suspicion of those days that he could not imagine that, although it was undoubtedly the case, they would salute him because he was a prominent member of island society.

Dr. Darling continues with his account from the Hospital:

'That evening the Junkers 52s began the first of their many trips to the airport. Amongst their passengers was a medical orderly plus his motorbike. He duly turned up at the General Hospital and said he had come to stay. Our Occupation had begun. For the first two or three months the Germans were content to leave their wounded in civilian hands. Mr. Halliwell had no time for the enemy, but he, in acceptance of the Geneva Convention never withheld his surgical skill from the German wounded being nursed on our wards.

My father recalls:

When the Germans arrived I was interviewed by the Senior Medical Officer for the region who spoke perfect English and, in fact held a degree of a local university. He said that of course they would not interfere with the hospital, but would I mind if they sent in any accident or any case of sickness which may turn up. They could, of course, be nursed amongst our patients. 'We are Germans and you are English, but we are both doctors.' My answer was 'Of course.' The impression I got was that this was a temporary arrangement as the war was nearly over and they did not expect any emergencies. He also asked if they could borrow some instruments and I learned that the young doctor in charge of the troops did not even have a pair of scissors or forceps. Their excuse was that the advance was so rapid that they did not have time to collect supplies. He also asked for accommodation for the young doctor who would live in and look after their patients. He was, in fact, unqualified.

In those early days all the Germans who came in were under the care of the local staff and, as ACH explains, "the German doctor and the young hospital resident doctors mixed quite freely in the doctors' room." At this stage, my father helped them and co-operated fully with them.

But matters were to change dramatically:

On August 25th the airport was bombed and there were six German casualties. They were admitted to hospital in a small ward of six beds. As their casualties increased so they took over more wards. Some of their casualties resulted from our bombing, and some from air crashes.

Nurse Keane tells how it felt to be nursing in this situation:

One morning I came in early on duty and noticed that something very unusual had happened in the wards. Instead of the usual first reading of the reports to me, Josie related the tidings of the night. Around midnight she was startled by the sound of soldiers' boots on the stone corridor. A German doctor, accompanied by a very nervous young soldier greeted her with a click of heels and an outstretched hand. He spoke very little English, and, with the aid of a dictionary told her that the soldier was to be admitted with suspected appendicitis. She tried to tell him that there was no room in the hospital but then he did a round of the four wards and found a bed inside the door of one of them. Here in this small ward lay the victims of the German machine gunning. I went over to the ward and saw the young German lying there, screened off from the others, unable to understand a single word we were saying. He couldn't have been more than nineteen years of age; at this moment in time his parents didn't know whether he was alive or dead. He was indeed the first of many German patients I was to treat, and as I continued on my morning round, I was met with hostile glances and bitter reproaches. 'Why was the enemy being treated?' I was questioned time and again. I reminded them that the nursing of the sick knew no national boundaries, but they insisted that he was the enemy and should be treated as such. I assured them that I would try to have him removed to another ward, but I had no time to carry out this promise. The doctor of the night before had arrived with an interpreter, a German who had been a resident of the island. With a low bow and clicking of heels, the middle aged doctor introduced himself. After examining his patient, he said that he would like him to remain on a little longer for observation. Then Matron was summoned. That's when things began to get a bit dramatic. Having lost all her composure, she looked completely upset as she awaited her orders through the interpreter. All the wounded natives of the island in the ward had to be transferred to another ward. They put me in charge and gave me the task of recruiting other nurses as there were to be more admissions. The unfortunate wounded were now in a crowded ward. Matron, shocked and shaken, visibly trying to collect herself, reminded the doctor that there was an acute shortage of trained staff, that she needed me and could she not arrange to let him have junior nurses instead? The answer was a firm 'No.' The doctor bowed and clicked and simply added: 'It is the war, gnädige Frau.' The matron looked at me, her arms folded in helpless resignation, and left the ward. Porters got busy shifting the beds to a ward which was already full and before I knew where I was, I found myself there with the one German patient. I had to contact Mr. Halliwell and break the news to him about sharing the operating theatre with the enemy. 'This is terrible, nurse, terrible. What if there are emergencies for me?' he asked. 'Yes,' I thought, 'what would happen then? Would the invader be treated first? Would the medical profession keep their Hippocratic Oath?' Matron had informed him, he said, that I was to be in charge and indeed he was sorry to hear it. 'I'm very much afraid that this is only the beginning,' he added, in a murmur, not so much addressing me as talking to himself. 'Who knows what drastic measures these Germans will have recourse to next?'

However, since the British girls were nursing Germans, their officers were deeply suspicious of what they called "sabotage". Mary Le Sueur recalls having to syringe out the ears of a German airman armed with the enormous syringes used in those days:

We had to be extremely careful, if I had perforated an eardrum I could have been accused of sabotage. I remember how my husband John, a physiotherapist, found a German who had taken a piece of redundant equipment and blown himself up. That was a dangerous moment. They were very paranoid at first, later they relaxed a bit.

In Guernsey the branch of Boots the Chemist had a 'Booklovers' Library'. In due course the Secret Field Police came to search for seditious literature. They confiscated a large number of books. However, their interpreter, who had worked for a Hamburg drug wholesaler in civilian life, hearing of the need for drugs, managed to obtain £50,000 worth of supplies sent directly from Germany. These were distributed throughout all the Islands.

On Christmas Day Sinel recorded that :

In spite of all our fears, with a bit of saving, scheming or wrangling, mostly the latter, the general provision of festive cheer was nothing short of wonderful. Although poultry was scarce, the Germans consuming a great deal of it, and supplies from France almost unworthy of mention for some time now there had been a lot of secret pig killing, which meant that pork which was not sold by the legitimate butcher found its way to consumers.

He concluded that:

At the end of six months of occupation we find ourselves in much better circumstances than we dared hope for at the beginning. The Germans for the most part seem to be out to make a good impression, and there is no doubt that they respect the local population… There is little arrogance among the enemy and their boasts on arrival of a quick victory have given way to the hope that there will be an agreement of some sort before very long: many have voiced a desire to return home and it is surprising the number who show little interest in the Nazi party.

At the Hospital it was reported the health of Islanders seemed to have improved because of the reduction in the consumption of fat and sugar and the increase in the consumption of vegetables. This situation was not, however, to last for long as rations were becoming shorter.

Chapter 7
1941
Changes and Privations

In island homes, life continued as normally as circumstances allowed. The New Year began with a raft of regulations concerning societies and clubs; the Salvation Army was closed down, as were the Freemasons. The Masonic Temple was cleared of its furnishings which were removed to Berlin and put on exhibition there.

The rationing of foodstuffs continued, and supplies became increasingly dependent on imports from the French mainland. In his official history of the Occupation, *The German Occupation of the Channel Islands*, Charles Cruickshank records how the first imports had arrived late in 1940, and had to be paid for in part by exports from the Island of potatoes and tomatoes. By the following year bread rationing began with $4^{1/2}$ pounds per adult per week and by 1945 it was to be reduced to one pound. In 1941 rationing of potatoes also began at 7 pounds a week for adults, dropping to 5 pounds. Meat rationing began at 12 ounces a week and dropped to a theoretical one ounce a week in 1945.

Obviously, those who had land grew what they could, and in the country people naturally fared much better than in the town. 'Le Clos du Chemin' possessed a large garden and ACH with his gardener, Mr. Newbery, were able to grow much of what they needed.

An order was issued that on 23rd June traffic was to change from driving on the left to driving on the right. Sinel commented: "This led to many complications, but it was surprising how soon we got used to it." My father told me that on the day of the changeover he ran over a German soldier. When I asked him whether he could have avoided him, he gave me one of his quizzical looks and replied, "Perhaps I could have!" A young Jersey cyclist who had obediently changed over to cycling on the right-hand side had the bizarre experience of colliding with a group of cycling German soldiers, who had apparently not received the message of the changeover.

One of the worst privations was the separation from families on the mainland. Early in 1941 the existing system of Red Cross messages to prisoners-of-war was extended to the Islands and the 'Bailiff of Jersey's Enquiry and News Service' handled many thousands of such messages until the Liberation. Conditions were strict, and regulations laid down that correspondents could write up to 25 words "on purely personal and family matters" on a Red Cross Message form. They were not to mention "service matters" or receipt of radio messages, results of enemy action or even names of towns. The message was to be posted to the International Red Cross in Geneva and forms could be obtained from local Citizens' Advice Bureaux. All letters were censored by the British and German authorities, and some of them had pieces cut out by the German censor. Cruickshank states that these messages "did no more than tell people that friends and relatives were still alive." In fact, my parents succeeded, not only in supporting each other with love and tenderness through this most difficult time, but they discussed our progress at school, business affairs, and made decisions about financial matters. They even managed, by cleverly designed codes, to share information about matters concerning the German occupying troops and the British military. All this was accomplished despite the fact that replies to any one message might take anything between two and four months to receive.

Early messages were mostly assurances of good health. The first batch of letters, with family news, sent from England at the end of 1940 and early the following year, reached Jersey in April, 1941. My father replied that life was going on much as usual, the estate was almost self supporting and that the Newberys were invaluable. They were all keeping cheerful, though life was rather dull. In February my mother sent "special thoughts for your birthday" which was the 22nd of the following month, and the letter arrived at the beginning of April, only ten days late. On 22nd March she wrote: "Dearest, Am sending this on your birthday. Wishing many happy returns and better days to come. All extremely well." He replied on 13th May: "Message arrived after Michael's birthday [8th May]. White cherry in full bloom. Am very well and busy in garden. All my love to you all." A further batch of letters arrived in August containing further family news and reflecting ACH's sense of humour, with comments like: "Hope Michael gets his scholarship, he will need it. All well here, but very bored, discomforts only minor. Producing all we need, except sherry; still have some left. Hope children don't change too much. I have not. You must not."

At the end of October another batch of letters passed through, Arthur replying: "Looking forward to marvellous holiday when this all over. You and children always in my thoughts. Using car sometimes [implying shortage of petrol]. Operated on Avarne and Ferguson [two colleagues]. Still some private work. Try send surgical gloves through Red Cross. Dozen if possible. Keeping up reasonable standard of living. Farm flourishing. Rabbits, fowls, ducks. Had a pig but it died. Plenty of vegetables." The requests for surgical gloves came regularly: the suppliers, Allen and Hanbury, despatched them via the Red Cross, and they eventually arrived. The story of the pig is recorded in a contemporary poem, reproduced below (author unknown, but possibly John Lewis!)

On 28th October my father showed in what he wrote how much he was missing us all. Referring to the day of the evacuation, he said: "Little in house altered since that day. Richard's toys still lying about. Michael's notices still on doors." In fact, the "notices on doors" were crossed Union Jacks pinned to the top lintel of the bedroom. One day a German soldier came in to look over the house for billeting purposes, came up the stairs, paused, looked at the two flags, made no comment and passed on.

With winter approaching he wrote: "Tennis court gives us hot baths" implying that the clinker from the cooker, which had been placed on the site of the unfinished tennis court as hardcore, was being reused as fuel, probably by soaking it in tar. This was a clear indication that fuel was getting short. However, he was "Very well and as cheerful as possible under circumstances. Just waiting."

THE SURGEON AND THE PIG OR (A FANTASY BASED ON FACT).

THERE IS A SURGEON OF RENOWN
WHO LIVES NOT FAR OUTSIDE THE TOWN,
A FELLOW MEDICO HE MET,
WHO LIVED A LITTLE FURTHER YET.
THEY TALKED OF THIS, THEY TALKED OF THAT,
THE LACK OF BREAD, OF MILK, OF FAT,
OF WHAT THE FARMERS DID WITH CREAM,
AND WHAT WAS EVERYBODY'S DREAM,
A SIDE OF PIG, A LEG OF PORK —
AND HERE'S THE OUTCOME OF THAT TALK

THE MEDICO RANG UP WITH GLEE,
TO SAY HE'D BOUGHT A P.I.G.
A FARMER WHO WAS LIVING NEAR,
HAD LET HIM HAVE IT — RATHER DEAR
ONE BUYS ONE'S THINGS IN OTHER WAYS.
A FREE TREATMENT FOR CHRONIC GOUT,
A COUSIN NEEDED TONSILS OUT;
IF THE SURGEON WOULD JUST OPERATE
THE FARMER WOULD CO-OPERATE.

THEY FED THE PIG FROM TAIL TO SNOUT,
AND NOT A WORD HAD GOT ABOUT.
THEY WAITED MONTHS TILL TIME WAS RIPE,
TILL JOINTS WERE JOINTS AND TRIPE WAS TRIPE.
BUT 'ERE THE DAY FOR SLAUGHTER CAME,
THE MEDICO RANG UP AGAIN,
I FEAR OUR PIG IS NOT TOO WELL,
WHAT AILS THE BEAST I CANNOT TELL,
IF YOU CAN BRING SYRINGE AND DRUGS,
I'LL HAVE HOT BOTTLES HERE AND RUGS".

A VET WOULD BE OF NO AVAIL,
HE'D SIMPLY THROW THEM INTO JAIL.
THEY RACKED THEIR BRAINS, THEY USED THEIR SKILL
BUT THE PIG WAS VERY, VERY ILL.
LAST WEEK HE LOOKED SO FAT AND SLEEK,
NOW HE WAS THIN AND VERY WEAK,
A KINDER DEATH HAD BEEN IN STORE ——
THEN THIS SLOW LINGERING AT THE DOOR
OF DEATH — WHICH MEANT A BIT OF LIME
INSTEAD OF CHOPS OR LEGS OR CHIME.

HOT BOTTLES, RUGS, SYRINGE DEFIED
IN SPITE OF ALL THEIR PIG HAD DIED.
THEY DECIDED ON A P.M.E.
TO FIND WHAT CAUSE OF DEATH COULD BE.
WAS IT PNEUMONIA OR A CHILL,
HAD CAUSED THEIR PIG TO FALL SO ILL?
THEY TRIED WITH ALL THEIR MIGHT AND MAIN
TO FIND WHAT HAD CAUSED THE PAIN.
THE CARCASE THEY THEN HID AWAY,
THEY HAD NO LUNCH FOR EASTER DAY.

Children of the Occupation

When I went to see her at her home in Wiltshire many years later, Audrey Goodwin (née Lock) recalled:

When the evacuation took place we were living in St. Helier. Everybody was rushing about, but my mother must have had a consultation and decided that we would stay. She was already working at 'Le Clos du Chemin' and a few weeks after the evacuation we moved in there. It was really nice living there, it was just as if it was my own house. I remember finding all the children's toys and saying to myself that I wished they were still there, and there would be someone to be friendly with.

However, there were quite a number of children who had not left, and she soon made friends, and got to know our neighbours Jean and Ray Fairlie, Wyshe Read, and Marion Michel, (now Sutton), daughter of farmer J.B. Michel. Later they all went to the Jersey Ladies' College together.

Audrey told me how desperately my father missed us children, and felt that much of the kindness he showed her and her friends helped in some way to compensate:

I remember Mr. Halliwell and Dr. Oliver, who had come to live with us, being really kind to me. One year, for my birthday they gave me a gold pencil with my name inscribed on it. I suppose because they didn't have their own children there, they were kind to me. I would describe Mr. Halliwell as a really nice person, kind and gentle, a true gentleman. He seemed always the same, and I never saw him being angry. And so was Dr. Oliver; he was somewhat gruff, but I was really fond of him.

Audrey actually has the happiest memories of her Occupation childhood:

When I think back on my childhood in Jersey it is always summer. In the big house at the bottom lived Dr. Drécourt, with his son James. I used to go down to the beach with Nancy O'Neill, and other friends. We used to meet in a big crowd. The first to arrive would dump their stuff and we would spend the day there swimming, and go home in time for curfew.

Nancy recalls one occasion when the two of them went swimming at Bel Royal:

We took our dog with us. Then we saw that the dog had gone home and two German officers were looking at our clothes. They tried to engage us in conversation, but we didn't respond. I expect they were missing their children, but you couldn't risk being friendly.

In the early years, before St. Ouen's beach was closed, Dr. Oliver and ACH used to take the girls surfing there.

Audrey also had parties in the house:

I had a few birthday parties at 'Le Clos du Chemin', two in the dining room and a couple in the nursery. The Fairlies used to come over from next door. I can't remember if I had a birthday cake, but I didn't feel deprived, because if you can't have it you soon get used to doing without it. We didn't go to the pictures, but we did go roller skating - the yard at the back of the house was a good place for that! There was nothing in the shops, but after two or three years it just seemed the norm.

Audrey's friend Nancy Alexandre (née O'Neill)) used to come up to 'Le Clos du Chemin' after school. She recalls:

I would usually take the short cut up the pathway which adjoined the property and walking up through the garden would see Mr. Halliwell working in the rock garden, giving him a respectful greeting as I passed by. I seem to remember him planting out flowers in red, white and blue. The children's nursery was a special place of wonder to me, and Audrey and I used to enjoy working through the contents of the toy boxes which lined one of the walls under the cushioned bench seat.

Up the road Marion Sutton had got used to living under Occupation conditions. She told me how her walk up the hill from school was sometimes perilous:

Sometimes the Germans would come down the steep hill from our house with their wagons and horses, and deliberately drive towards me so that I would have to scramble up the hedge. As far as food was concerned I was lucky, because we lived on a farm, but my parents were not the kind of people who believed in keeping masses of milk back. I used to go to some farms where you had whipped cream and butter. Although we had a farm we didn't live richly. We used to kill a pig now and then; you weren't allowed to do that. We used to have an illicit pig, which you had to hide. Then came the problem of killing it. When it was being killed I remember the men banging on corrugated iron so that the Germans nearby wouldn't hear. One night when we had just killed a pig, when my mother was rendering some fat on the cooker, an officer came in, as he often did, when their electricity was off, to sit in the kitchen and write letters. He sat at one end of the kitchen table and my mother at the other. She didn't dare do anything about the fat for fear he would get up and have a look.

As children we didn't have any dealings with the Germans direct. But they were all round the farm. In one of the fields I had a disused chicken hut which I used as a play house. A friend of mine used to come for weekends; and we would go inside and pretend it was night. Outside the hut was a big tree and one day we heard the sound of feet nearby and found that one of the soldiers was spending a penny against our tree. We were terrified and rooted to the spot. We were sure they would have shot us if they had found us. We must have stayed there for a good five minutes after they had gone.

Marion told me how she was going to school by bus at first, but that a decision was made that they would have to cycle. Most of the parents were against this so about ten of them found themselves attending a private school at the house of Mr. and Mrs. Read, 'The Hollies'. The teaching arrangements were somewhat haphazard. Marion explains:

We had a woman who came and taught us in the morning and then one afternoon she would come and take us sketching and another afternoon we all trooped down to Mrs. Romeril's in Beaumont to do sewing. Another afternoon Mrs. Read took us for cookery, we did things like bottling fruit. Another afternoon we would go to Harry Ballantine and do dramatic art. We did some Shakespeare which was way above my head. I was only seven and the other girls were in their teens. He asked us to learn 'All the world's a stage...' I took it home and worked at it; I still remember it.

Alastair Fairlie remembers being taught elocution by Harry Ballantine, who always had a large glass of gin by his side. The lessons went on until about 4 o'clock, at which time the children were hustled out of the way, and my father and other neighbours arrived to share Harry's bottle of gin.

Marion explained how things turned out:

By the end of the year the parents got together and decided it was safe for us to cycle to school. That was all right until the tyres started to wear out. We used up our energy going to and from school. We had to learn German at school and we were fortunate in that we had our own teachers. We did small plays and the German officers used to come and listen to them. We learnt songs, too: we didn't mind that, it was just part of school life.

A Case of Tuberculosis

A Quiet Place is the title of a book written by Peggy Boléat about her Occupation experiences. For several years she was in the care of ACH when suffering from tuberculosis. Her story begins in 1935 when she suffered from persistent pain in her right buttock and down the leg. Her doctor, Pat Gallagher, an Irishman of much charm and blarney, suggested muscle strain and prescribed rest, but she came to find she could not move. She was hospitalised briefly in the small cottage Hospital, the Dispensary, and this brought some relief, but she always walked with a limp. Five years later, her doctor having died, she had a recurrence of the pain and her new doctor, Dr. Gow, a man of ample proportions and avuncular manner, hearing her symptoms, without examining her, said:

"Lassie, girls of your age don't have sciatica, I'm referring you to Mr. Halliwell at the General Hospital."

The year 1941 was to introduce her to ACH and commit her to a long and ultimately successful stay in hospital with tuberculosis. Peggy takes up the story:

"The clinic Ruby [her stepmother] and I attended at the General Hospital in St. Helier was held by Mr. Halliwell, the Consultant Surgeon. It was my second visit. This time I would know the result of my X-rays and the skin test I had been given less than an hour ago. …It was two o'clock. Mr. Halliwell had arrived, on the minute.

I should describe Mr. Halliwell. He was the Consultant Surgeon at the General Hospital and I was one of his patients. He was a tall, thin man, with a fair complexion. Immaculate would be the word which explains the chief impression he gave. This impression was emphasised by the light grey suits of fine cloth that he wore and by his glasses, which seemed to gleam cleanliness. He fitted exactly my idea of how a surgeon should look. Despite possessing great charm, of which he later showed a little, he was also aloof as befitted the exalted position held by surgeons in those days.

The clinic was open and Ruby and I were the first to be called into the surgery. The dark red stain on the inside of my forearm… showed a positive reaction to the skin test I had received. It confirmed the diagnosis that I was suffering from tuberculosis. Mr. Halliwell came straight to the point. 'You have TB of the right sacro-iliac joint and will have to come into hospital and spend a year in a plaster cast, on your back.' I looked at him as if I hadn't heard. 'When will you come in?' 'On Monday.' Was it really I, answering the question in such a matter of fact way? I must have looked stunned, because Ruby patted me on my hand as she whispered to me 'It's going to be all right.' As we left the hospital I glanced up at the clock above the entrance. It was ten minutes past two. On the way home I wondered why I had given myself only one week's grace. No doubt Mr. Halliwell used a psychological approach to patients such as I. His question 'When will you come in?' had demanded an answer, not prevarication. I realised that the timing of his question was masterly, leaving me no time to think or ask the opinions of others.

The Hospital had laid in a good stock of Celona bandages used for making plaster casts. However, there were problems as ACH explains:

When the Germans arrived our Celona bandages were quite new to them and they asked for some. They were so insistent that the Theatre Sister could not refuse and we had to clear out all our stock and leave it, for safe custody, at the houses of various doctors, or they would have taken it all. When these were finally used up, we made plaster beds, etc., out of book muslin and builders' plaster. But they were not very good.

On the 8th June 1941, Peggy presented herself at the porter's desk and was shown to her ward. The following morning she was taken to theatre to have a plaster cast made. She was told that she would have home-made plaster bandages because the normal ones were no longer available. She lay face down on the operating table. She explains what happened next:

To hand were three buckets standing on the floor. The first held loosely rolled gauze bandages, the second plaster of Paris and the third water. The method was to shake a bandage in the plaster of Paris then plunge it into the water and pass it quickly to Mr. Halliwell. He unwound each plaster bandage back and forth across my back and legs until sufficient density was built up to hold a rigid shape... When the plaster was finished everyone went off for coffee and I was left in the theatre to 'dry off a bit.'... Mr. Halliwell returned and expressed himself satisfied with the plaster. It was retained for further drying and I was taken back to the ward.

After a short while Peggy was moved to Overdale Hospital, an old style isolation hospital outside St. Helier in a beautiful setting overlooking St. Aubin's Bay. She is critical of the custom of those days of not telling patients much about their condition:

Mr. Halliwell made quarterly visits. The first of these since leaving the General Hospital had been in October when my X-ray was arranged. If, on his visit, he had sat down and discussed my illness with me, I would not have felt so let down. Instead, accompanied by Sister, he spoke to me for a few minutes on inconsequential subjects, Sister told me I was doing very well, he smiled charmingly, and they moved away. Etiquette prevented me from asking any pertinent questions of Mr. Halliwell. I could only ask Sister if she would ask for me. It went much further than that. Should one wish to ask Sister about a less important matter, one should first ask a staff nurse if she would approach Sister. Many months later I took great pleasure in breaking with this tradition.

Hospital Wards Commandeered

On the wards Mauyen Keane was getting used to helping nurse German patients, having been drafted in by the Army medical authorities much to the chagrin of the Matron. Early in 1941 there was a change, as the Army, who had been in place for six months, were replaced by the Air Force. Nurse Keane explains:

There was a little ceremony in the corridor as the departing doctor introduced us to the new doctor from the Luftwaffe; he had high praise for our efficiency and dedication to nursing. Our new doctor was a kind, grey haired man who was well able to speak good English, even though he never did so on the wards. In the nurses' office he would occasionally speak about the awful futility of war. 'We are fighting our cousins,' he would exclaim. This came as quite a surprise to us, as we'd been asked by the army doctor not to speak of the war.

Shortly after this, hearing an unusually long discussion in the corridor, Nurse Keane went to the nurses' office to discover that the Matron, Miss Millar, had resigned. She was spared the next big upheaval when the Germans took over the female surgical ward on the opposite floor, also containing the main Operating Theatre and all the acute medical and surgical wards, male and female. On 23rd April Miss M.A.L. Carter was appointed in her place.

As part of the island defences, the Germans had sown land mines along the coasts. Although these were clearly marked, sometimes stray animals or even children and adults would set them off. Amélie Rogon and her two children lived at Fliquet. I went to see her and she told me that her husband, who was of French birth, had served with the Free French under General de Gaulle. Their elder child, John, loved to go low water fishing and on 16th March he went with his mother and younger sister, six-year old Simone. However, tragically, Simone wandered from the pathway and trod on a landmine. The huge explosion alerted the neighbouring troops. Although injured herself, Madame Rogon carried her daughter, badly injured, but still alive, up the road. They were all taken by a German ambulance to the Hospital, where they were admitted and needed their wounds stitching. Sister Renouard who was in charge of the children's ward later told Simone she came in "looking like a little dying soldier." ACH was called to see Simone whose left leg was "hanging off" and her right side and shoulder were badly damaged. Fortunately, she had been wearing a small pair of Wellingtons which had protected her slightly from the blast. She remembers the enormous trouble he took in repairing her right leg and foot; he was, she recalls, "a tremendous surgeon." Altogether Simone was in hospital for many months, but she made a complete recovery, and over sixty years later walks perfectly normally. The Rogon family were remarkably lucky, for several months later another land mine exploded, at La Rocque, killing two soldiers.

In July, my father received perhaps the biggest blow of his whole career, as he explains:

Early in July 1941 the German Commandant ordered the whole of the first floor, including the main theatre, should be taken over by the Germans and we were given forty-eight hours in which to move. Through Dr. McKinstry we protested to Graf von Schmettow, the Civil Commandant, and he agreed that our protests were just and withdrew the order. But two days later it was re-imposed on the orders of the military Governor on instructions from Berlin, and all our patients were moved to the Maternity Ward which later became the Children's Unit. Here fortunately we had an operating theatre and these quarters were used for the rest of the war.

Due to wartime restrictions on movement there were special problems for expectant mothers. It so happened that on the other side of town was the other small hospital, the Jersey Dispensary, which had been closed following the evacuation of its medical staff and some of its nursing staff. As ACH explains:

When the Germans arrived their orders contained so many restrictions upon night traffic and zones around the coasts into which civilians could not go at night, that it was decided by Dr. McKinstry to reopen the former Jersey Dispensary and Infirmary as a Maternity Hospital and advise all maternity cases to come in the Hospital in good time so as to avoid any incidents which might occur if any midwives had to go into the military zones at night. The hospital was re-opened on July 24th when the Matron was Miss Thornley, with one Sister, Sister Bissell, a King's College Hospital Sister who was convalescing in Jersey at the time the Germans took over, and one other nurse. The first baby was born on the 29th. Further staff joined them, including Sister Dorey and the hospital was kept fully occupied during the whole of the war. Sister Bissell later came to the General Hospital as Sister Tutor in July 1943.

The changeover is described in Dr. Darling's account:

This empty hospital now became the island's maternity unit and into it we transferred our maternity patients and maternity nurses. The children's ward on the ground floor remained as before. Into the empty wards we moved all the female patients, medical and surgical, from the wards of the first floor of the main building. 'Top floor' contained long term chronic sick, and these were transferred either to the chronic sick wards at the back of the hospital or to 'Sandybrook' - an empty house just below 'Le Clos du Chemin' which was hurriedly made ready for its new function. Our acute male patients moved up to top floor and that completed what was a traumatic and grievous changeover. It was far from ideal but we adjusted and settled down with all the problems brought on by shortages of every kind and a gradually increasing level of malnutrition. Mr. Halliwell remained the vital centre of all our activity. To us all he was a faithful friend and mentor. We liked him, trusted him and respected him. We could not imagine the hospital without him. He never despaired and always faced up to each new challenge with confident optimism. He set the example and we all did our best to follow.

Later he saw the gaseous anaesthetics run out but continued to operate using only local anaesthetics and spinal anaesthetics or ether and chloroform. It was fascinating to watch him do major abdominal surgery using only local or spinal anaesthetics. Most patients preferred to be asleep and they received an intravenous injection of 'Sedabins', a mixture of morphine and hyoscene. Even if their level of consciousness remained reasonably high they were sedated and calm and remembered nothing of their ordeal. He adjusted to the use of home made plaster of Paris bandages which set slowly and required much reinforcement. He tolerated the use of strange suture materials and adjusted the number of his stitches. He was always available on the 'phone and never rejected the slightest suggestion that his presence would be appreciated. During my almost six years in the hospital I had five weeks' leave and twelve weeks away with diphtheria and rheumatic fever. During those seventeen weeks he always came to live in my quarters thus providing 24 hour resident medical cover.

ACH explains how they managed:

All the anaesthetics were held at the hospital and any outside doctor had to draw from us after satisfying us that an anaesthetic was really necessary. Ether ran out in 1943 but we had plenty of chloroform and percaine for spinal anaesthetics. All anaesthetics were used very carefully and as many as possible were done under local or spinal.

Betty Thurban recalls the make do and mend:

Early on we had a lot of difficulty continuing with malt and cod liver oil for children. Malt came from the breweries and some of the merchants were able to give us some cod liver oil. When we ran out of the cod liver oil, the occupying forces gave us fish livers which were steamed by our chemist down in the basement. Rumour had it that we were feeding our patients on rotten fish, because the smell was pretty appalling. Other important drugs too were not available, thyroid, needed by many patients, came from animals' thyroid glands which was given to the hospital from the abattoirs. Skin conditions were another great problem. We had an enormous number of cases, partly because of the food, lack of vitamins, and also scabies because of the lack of soap. This led to a second condition known as 'Occupation dermatitis' in which all the warm areas of the body developed pustules. The only way to treat it was to scrub the arms and hands, and then use tar ointment. It looked and smelt awful!

Colleagues but Enemies

One afternoon in December, 1941 Nurse Keane reported an unusual occurrence, bringing together two colleagues to face each other from opposite sides of the fence:

An orderly raced past me and then turned back breathlessly to ask me to get the English surgeon to the operating theatre immediately. The resident doctor had been in a car crash and had asked for Mr. Halliwell. As to the nature of the accident the orderly had no idea, and as I made my way upstairs to the civilian wards, I imagined the reaction of the overworked surgeon. They had already taken his wards and demanded that they share his operating theatre; now they were looking for treatment.

'They have their own doctors,' he exclaimed, 'why me?' There was nothing I could add to what I had already been ordered to tell him. He fell into silence for a minute or two. He wasn't going to wait until being ordered at gunpoint so he said: 'Tell them I don't want any retinue nurse. Tell them I shall work alone with you.' When we reached the door of the operating theatre, Mr. Halliwell stood outside while I managed to persuade the two German doctors standing over the patient to leave the theatre. I was relieved to see that the patient had only a lacerated upper lip. Then Mr. Halliwell entered, bidding the patient a cool 'Good afternoon' and proceeded to inspect the lip. He turned abruptly to scrub up while I prepared for stitching. As he finished the neat stitches, the patient asked for a 'Spiegel' (mirror), unable to articulate the word very clearly. When I translated to Mr. Halliwell, the surgeon exclaimed sarcastically: 'A mirror, nurse! On my operating table!' He looked very indignant. 'Oh ha', said the Air-Force doctor on the table in English, 'I am more beautiful now, as before.' He lay there inspecting his stitched lip with satisfaction. But the face of the healer retained its own stiff upper lip - and even now more so than before. I must say I was quite amused at the German's reaction to the operation but I tried not to show it to the Englishman. The patient extended his hand in a gesture of gratitude, but Mr. Halliwell, his gloves now discarded, kept his hands firmly behind his back. 'That's quite all right,' he responded glibly, 'good afternoon,' and he made his way briskly to the exit.

I really felt sorry for that German doctor who clearly found the war as tragic and useless as his English fellow professional. 'My own profession' he said, sadly 'and he would not take my hand.' I tried to reassure him that the English surgeon was acting in appalling circumstances forced upon him and the rest of us by the Germans and then I asked him why he had requested to be treated by Mr. Halliwell in the first place. 'I thought I might get to know him' was all he replied.

As can be seen from the above, ACH had strong views about fraternisation. He wrote:

As far as the nursing staff were concerned there was very little fraternisation. The Jersey nurses treated the Germans with cold courtesy. Some of the Irish nurses were not quite so particular, no doubt their feelings were not quite the same as ours, as Southern Ireland was not at war with Germany. Only two Irish nurses became really friendly with the Germans, one of whom married a German doctor. I was very bitter about it at the time - rather foolishly perhaps.

The Irish nurse referred to above is Nurse Keane, who married and went to live in Germany, eventually moving with her husband back to Ireland at the end of hostilities. This sad little incident serves to highlight the tremendous pressures put upon fellow professionals by the conflict in which they were caught up. Who knows what that German doctor might have gained by really getting to know my father? However, ACH is known as one who would never shake the hand of a German. Obviously, he was incensed by the actions of the Germans in taking over a large part of his hospital and its principal operating theatre. He was forced to make do with a small maternity theatre for the duration, and all his surgery for the five years was carried out there. It seems likely that his attitude did not go unnoticed, and when towards the end of the war he offered to help care for the many German casualties brought back from St. Malo he was deeply hurt when his offer of professional help was unceremoniously refused.

However, there was co-operation at some levels. One day a young Jerseyman was admitted with severe burns, and as the local people did not have the wherewithal to treat him properly, the Germans agreed to take him on their ward. On his discharge he expressed his gratitude. The German doctor replied: "Don't thank me, dear boy, thank Adolf Hitler and the Third Reich."

During the year, rations for the civilian population were reduced and Dr. McKinstry reported:

The main fact is that as things are at present, nobody is getting sufficient or a balanced diet. It is short in total calories and relatively deficient in fats and first class proteins.

He also reported that deaths from tuberculosis were 50% above the UK national average and predicted an increase in maternal and infant deaths.

According to Sinel, the end of 1941 "finds us quite cheerful and quietly optimistic for the next twelve months, although local conditions have greatly deteriorated; there is a lot to be thankful for, however, and in spite of the usual grouses, which are inevitable in times like these, about the local authorities, there is no doubt that, in his own mind, everyone feels they are doing their best… The Germans appear to be very depressed and they are all wishing for a quick finish to the war… Thousands of foreign workers - directed by the Todt Organisation - are being poured into the Island… The general health as a whole is quite good, but there have been many cases of diarrhoea or colitis, which is thought to be due to the bread."

The *Organisation Todt* was a para-military labour organisation in which thousands of "undesirables" were employed, often in appalling conditions, for the building works of the *Reich*. Amongst these were people of Jewish extraction, Slavic people, alleged Communists, homosexuals, and the like. Their arrival was to give Islanders a view of another side of Nazism, in stark contrast to the fairly benevolent face they had observed hitherto.

Maternity

John Lewis, who was responsible for the newly founded Jersey Maternity Hospital in St. Saviour's Road, St. Helier, recalls the "very high sense of duty and comradeship amongst the staff, led by the matron Miss Elizabeth Thornley who kept the same staff for the whole of the five years, with very few exceptions. All through that time there was no talk of hours of work or overtime. If there was work to be done, it was done, and properly, no matter how long it took. Everyone worked for love of the job, and with very little thought of remuneration."

Dr. Lewis remembers calling ACH to see a tiny baby with a strangulated hernia:

Our senior surgeon, Mr. Arthur Halliwell FRCS, was called in, and had no luck either [in putting the hernia back]. Immediate operation was imperative for, although the baby might well die during the operation, he would certainly die if it were not done.

With some trepidation I gave the anaesthetic, and marvelled at the deftness of Mr. Halliwell's fingers working in such a tiny space. All through his working life he was noted for his speed and delicate touch. When the baby was returned to his cot, still unconscious, he looked like a small, wax doll, but he was still alive.

On another occasion John Lewis found himself asked by the German Medical Officer to provide ante-natal facilities for two Russian women. Apparently, they were but newly married when the men in their village were being rounded up for the labour organisation. They had succeeded in disguising themselves as males so as not to be separated from their husbands. In due course they were both delivered of healthy babies. All went well, but there seemed to be a problem. They needed baby clothes. The *Organisation Todt* put an advertisement in the *Evening Post* and local people rallied round. But apparently the Russian mothers did not think much of these tiny vests and matinée coats. They would hold them up and explode with laughter. They were only satisfied when, by the use of sign language, they succeeded in explaining that they wanted old sheets and blankets. These they then tore into strips and sewed them end to end in lengths of three or four metres, and then proceeded to wrap each baby into a small cocoon, with their arms by their sides, leaving only a small aperture at the front for the face and at the back for changing. Lewis comments:

Why the babies did not die of heat stroke I cannot imagine. I could quite see it would make sense in Central Russia, with the temperature at forty degrees below zero, but at this particular time the Island was enjoying a mini heat-wave. I worried about this quite a lot and tried to communicate my concern to the mothers, …but they were completely adamant and left hospital with their babies still tightly cocooned, seemingly still well and thriving.

Lewis records that they had about two thousand deliveries in the five years, with no infections to speak of, and only three maternal deaths, of which two were inevitable. He also refers to those cases where local girls had babies by German fathers. He estimated that the numbers were not more than a hundred. He reckons that, although at the time the mothers were stigmatised as "Jerrybags", "whatever stigma was originally attached to them is completely forgotten, and those of them that I know personally are good, solid, well respected Jersey citizens."

Perhaps all was not quite as simple as that, for in my 25 years as Rector at St. Brelade I heard certainly of two cases where a life ended in suicide. He is, however, probably correct when he concludes:

A conquering army, from time immemorial has always brought a change of blood, and in Jersey's case this will I am sure have done no harm in the long run.

The Jersey General Hospital. Although the Hospital has been greatly extended and modernised since the war, the original façade onto Gloucester Street is largely unchanged. *Robin Briault*

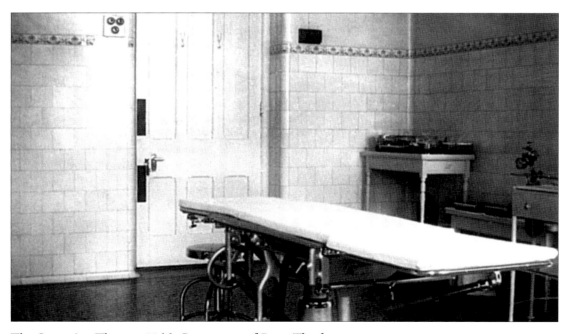

The Operating Theatre, 1946. *By courtesy of Betty Thurban*

Dr. Noel McKinstry. *By courtesy of Health and Social Services*

Dr. John Hanna. *CIOS Collection*

Dr. Harold Blampied.

Hospital staff on the steps of the General Hospital in May, 1945.
(From the front) Nurses S. Marquis, C. Foot, ? Germain and Mr. Hornby.
The German sign on the right reads 'KR' = 'Krankenhaus', 'ABTLG II' = 'Abteilung II' (Section II),
'1 Stock' = '1st Floor'. *CIOS Collection*

Hospital staff, June, 1945. In the centre is Dr. McKinstry with Matron Carter; Dr. Darling is second from the left, and ACH fourth from the left; fourth from the right is Dr. Blampied, and Mr. Osmont is second from the right. *By courtesy of Health and Social Services*

A group of nurses with a patient (Mr. Greeney), May, 1945. (L to R) Nurse R. Griffin, Nurse N. Houillebecq, Staff Nurse J. Mines (Acting Sister), Staff Nurse V. Cavey, Nurse S. Millow, Nurse M. Boucheré and Nurse D. Lamy. *By courtesy of Michael Ginns*

Dr. Hanna with Student Nurse Bastin, and Student Nurse Le Corre, 1946.
By courtesy of Betty Thurban

Student Nurse Le Corre, Staff Nurse Marquis and Sister Le Seelleur, 1946.
By courtesy of Betty Thurban

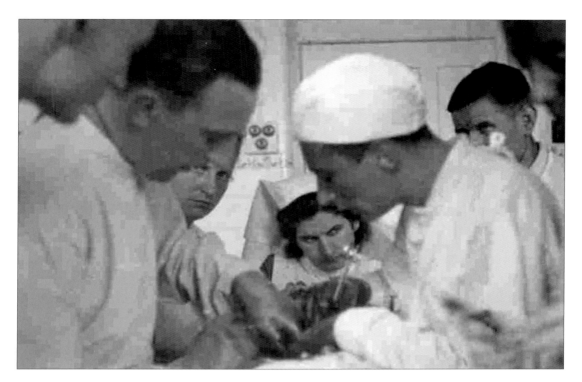

Scene in the Operating Theatre. Nurse Keane is in the centre, whilst Dieter Rosenstock looks on, at the far left. *By courtesy of Gabriel Rosenstock*

Hospital staff with two members of the Royal Army Medical Corps on the steps of the main entrance, May, 1945. Amongst those in the picture with Ray Osmont, wearing the white coat, are Nurses Beaugie, Patch, Romeril, Manning, Le Seelleur, Le Maistre, Le Corre, Millow, Baudins, Jandron and Cudlipp, Matron Carter (holding the Pekinese), Staff Nurse Fanning and Sisters Corbin and Renouard. *By courtesy of Health and Social Services*

Chapter 8
1942
The Screw Tightens

My father began the year by reporting that all was well at home, they had had plenty of Christmas fare, "the farm" was flourishing and he still had some private work. He ended: "Looking forward to seeing you. My love, Arthur." That letter took only nine weeks to arrive and my mother reported that the Red Cross had sent twelve pairs of surgical gloves, adding: "Your cheerfulness is wonderful. It helps me."

In February my father recorded his thankfulness that winter was almost over. So far, it had been quite good. He had whiled the time away in the evenings playing billiards with his neighbours, the Fairlies, in the barn of neighbouring farmer J.B. Michel. He added that his chief occupation was household management, but he had succeeded in getting a credit balance. He ended: "Cannot think how you carry on."

My father, as Surgeon Lieutenant in the First World War, had spent his leisure time in HMS *Delhi* decoding the ciphers. In March he began introducing into his letters code words by which he could report on military matters. On 23rd March he wrote: "Do you remember Eccles. We are disappointed at seeing so little of his children in these days, but Ethel's father often sees them." It will be recalled that Dr. Eccles RN had visited us in 1940, and as he was serving in the armed services, his "children" must be a reference to the British military. "Ethel's father" was a Guernsey physician, so this may refer to the commando raids on that island, which took place the previous year, or some raid on installations in Guernsey by the RAF. Later the same month he wrote: "We see a lot of Mrs. Le Roux's children - quiet, well behaved, but looking forward as we do." Mrs. Le Roux was a German-Swiss lady who cleaned at 'Le Clos du Chemin', and had only one daughter. Her "children" must therefore refer to the German military. So the message was that behaviour amongst the occupying troops was good and well disciplined and that they, too, were fed up with the war and looking forwards to its end. This message ended with the request: "Write me care of Judge Hanna." This gentleman was the father of the local physician and lived in the Irish Republic. As Eire remained neutral throughout the war, it would logically be possible to correspond via a neutral country. A later letter gave his address. My mother made contact with him and notified ACH that the arrangement was in place with the words: "Judge Hanna flourishing." A letter was sent, but was eventually returned, having reached France, with the words "Pas de communications".

Through the months they discussed family progress, investments, inheritance, anniversaries, especially the June ones, two birthdays and their wedding anniversary.

In April, correspondence began about a way which my father had devised to send money to the family via Barclay's Bank. It must have involved him paying money to the local branch and my mother being given credit by Barclay's Head Office in London, because the letter instructed her to inquire there. Precisely how the message was conveyed to Barclay's in London is unclear.

Alexander Coutanche, in his memoirs, records that the message service which he set up with the assistance of the Red Cross was responsible for requests for certificates of births, marriages and deaths and "arranged for the transfer of money to relatives in Great Britain".

Mr. Colin Powell of the Jersey Financial Services Commission kindly agreed to look into the matter for me. Amongst papers on banking arrangements during the Occupation he found a reference to "Branch Records". The document states: "Insofar as possible Branch Records were reconstructed on the mainland." It is explained that in cases of claims by refugees and by dependants on the mainland of "imprisoned" Islanders, decisions were based "not on a narrowly legalistic - but on a broad and humane interpretation of their duties," adding "evidence of the great appreciation of refugees in this regard has not been lacking."

Mr. Powell concluded:

It would appear from this that accounts were held in the United Kingdom from which funds could be drawn to support the dependants of those who had remained on the Island, and who were then living in the United Kingdom. No doubt in many cases the instructions for drawing funds from the account were established at the outset. However, insofar as any new instructions were given these could only have been achieved through using banks in neutral third countries such as Switzerland or Portugal.

At the end of June, ACH reported: "Am sending more now I know it can be done. It should be useful." In July he wrote: "Have sent further two hundred. More will follow now scheme appears to work."

A Toast to Peace

At the Hospital, following the German takeover of the main Operating Theatre, pressures were building up and my father was feeling the strain. Supplies were running short and he reported that the surgical gloves which my mother had ordered had still not arrived. Though he was trying hard, he was finding it difficult to concentrate on his work.

Then an incident occurred in which a German doctor, speaking a language which my father understood, succeeded in momentarily bridging the gulf between the English and German surgeon. Nurse Keane explains:

… the Air Force was due to leave the Island and to be replaced by the Army. On the evening of the surgeon's departure, he came on the wards to say good-bye to us nurses. He presented us with a bottle of champagne and gave us another one to pass on to Mr. Halliwell. Champagne, together with all other luxuries, hadn't been seen on the Island since the Occupation.

He wished Mr. Halliwell would drink a toast to both of them and to peace. And so, armed with a bottle of champagne, I waited in the nurses' office until the evening rounds were over. Before I opened my mouth he was frowning as if in anticipation of some more bad news. 'No requests, this time, Mr. Halliwell,' I said, as I handed him the rare vintage. Then I relayed the message of goodwill. His tired eyes lit up when he saw the bottle; he was indeed visibly touched. He patted my head in paternal fashion and said, half absently, 'We have all been under a great strain nurse.' I could think of nothing else to say other than, 'It will all be over soon' and there and then I found myself firmly believing what I had just said, and, with a lighter heart, went quickly downstairs to nurse his enemies.

The changeover was to mean a total change of her life for Nurse Keane. Amongst the incoming troops was a doctor in charge from Berlin and a young German medical student, named Dieter Rosenstock. She explains:

Dieter and I worked a lot together in the operating theatre. He was always glad to be able to disguise his uniform with the green surgeon's theatre gown. Mr. Halliwell's all white gown stood out in sharp contrast to the dark green colours of the Germans.

At the end of June the couple got engaged. Although Hitler had forbidden any German marrying a foreigner, Mauyen was hopeful that her Irish nationality might give her exemption from this prohibition. In due course Dieter was posted back to Germany, managed to get Mauyen permission to travel to Germany, and she gave in her notice. She went to collect her diploma and comments: "Mr. Halliwell and Dr. Hanna signed it, but not without telling me they should be certifying me as insane for wanting to travel to Germany in the middle of a war." After a long journey Mauyen arrived safely at Dieter's home and the couple applied to marry. But first they had to have a racial check up, and Mauyen was turned down for marriage as she was deemed to have "a Jewish nose". In the event they were married secretly by a priest, and started a family.

On 7th April my father reported that he, with Dr. Blampied and Dr. McKinstry, had been appointed members of the Medical Trust for the Island.

Radio Receivers Banned

Hitler was immensely proud of his only British possessions and determined to make them an impregnable fortress which would remain German for all time. With the growth in the size of the fortifications there came a corresponding concern with security. Cruickshank reports that in March the *Geheimefeldpolizei* (Secret Field Police) in Jersey reported to the *Abwehr* (Military Counter Intelligence) HQ in France the disappearance of the entire extension plans of the Jersey *Luftwaffe* base. In response to the evident need for greater security thirteen extra Secret Field Police were despatched to the Channel Islands. In mid-April *Abwehr France* agreed to the need to confiscate all wireless sets in the Channel Islands because of the possibility of converting radio receivers into transmitters. They were also concerned about the danger of the occupying troops being influenced by hearing the BBC news. In Germany, from the outbreak of war, radio sets were allowed, but listening to the BBC was forbidden. In other occupied countries confiscation of radios had been abandoned as impractical.

Early in 1941 there arrived on the staff of the German civil affairs unit, *Feldkommandantur 515*, the German nobleman Hans Max von Aufsess who achieved a reputation as a "chivalrous foe" in the way in which he often intervened on behalf of the Islanders with his superiors in Germany. He was no Nazi and strongly resented anything which would present his people in an unfavourable light. He was to fight many battles in the cause of humanity and common sense. A countryman and lover of nature, he would visit those with German ancestry or occupiers of manor houses. These people came to be regarded for these reasons as collaborators because they "entertained the Germans". His contacts with such people were of a cultural and literary nature, and it could be argued that in the long term so called "entertainment of the Germans" was highly beneficial to the island population, because it gave those officers a taste of "normal life" and Jersey culture in an abnormal situation. From a perusal of von Aufsess's diary it is clear that, apart from his love of nature and his horses, his contacts with some of the manorial families, in particular Mrs. Riley at Rozel, and the Fieldings at Samarès, were his great relief from the tedium of army life, and may have been largely instrumental in strengthening his resolve to do his very best for the Islanders.

Von Aufsess fought a long and eventually losing battle against the ban on wireless sets, not least because he feared it would lead to a deterioration in relations with the civilian population who "had up to then acted in the most correct manner". He wrote of the Bailiff of Jersey:

Cold and vulpine visaged, …he is our sworn opponent, not so much because he hates us, he is too wily an old lawyer for that - as because he understandably chafes against the restriction to his authority and feels wounded in his self-esteem. It is easily foreseeable that in the future he will twist everything against us to his own glorification.

On the occasion of a visit he commented: "He probably thinks he can dominate me, but it is his vanity in this respect which gives me a hold over him. I have now had so much experience of conceit that I believe I know how to deal with it… He casts himself in the role of a saviour… Yet, such is his adroitness, experience and ability to adapt, that I really get on very well with him, and even hope in time to establish a more cordial relationship." Coutanche once said that, despite the situation, he could not help regarding von Aufsess as a friend. The Attorney-General, Duret Aubin, who had daily contact with him and probably bore the major burden of the administrative problems which had to be tackled on a daily basis, found in him a kindred spirit, as they were both Leica fans. One day, von Aufsess wistfully remarked that if it were not for this war, they could have been good friends.

In the end the combined power of combat troop commanders, counter-intelligence and the *Wehrmacht* High Command won through. Accordingly, on 6th June the Bailiff of Jersey was instructed to implement the order. By 22nd June 10,050 wireless sets were handed in. However, many were not, and the Germans were aware of this. Reporting this to the Military Governor in France they were told to impose sentences of up to six weeks' imprisonment and fines of £3,000. Later, they were told to give an order threatening the death sentence or alternatively heavier prison sentences. This ruling put an intolerable strain on the populace who had not only to be alert to the random searches of the military but (much more difficult) to take account of the risk of being betrayed by their own people if it became known that they had access to sources of news. In fact, despite the courageous activities of Post Office staff who intercepted as many letters as they could, a steady flow of denunciations reached the German authorities who were, it was reported, actually embarrassed by the apparent readiness of Jersey people to betray their kith and kin to pay off old scores. In some cases betrayal meant a lingering death in a concentration camp.

For some time my father had had a direct telephone line to the Hospital in case of emergencies. In the event it was not really required, so he had it cut several hundred yards from the house and turned it into a very effective aerial for the crystal set which had replaced his surrendered radiogram. He used to listen to it in bed before starting the day's work. One morning, however, the Germans came to search the house, so he jumped out of bed, and threw the bedclothes over the offending instrument, which was not discovered.

At the Hospital one of the patients of Betty Thurban (née Le Corre), who had a knee problem and was barely able to walk, became very agitated on hearing the news of an impending house to house search for illegal radios. As there was no longer any civilian transport available it was agreed that an ambulance be called and 'Nurse Le Corre' was instructed to take the patient to his home and wait in the ambulance while he hid his radio.

Up the lane at 'Wheatlands', the farm of our neighbours the Michels, a nerve-wracking search was carried out by the Germans. Someone reported that they had a radio in the house and the military came to look for it. They were exceedingly thorough and demanded to see the loft. They searched high and low and came to a cupboard, which actually contained the radio. Asked to open the cupboard, J.B. Michel said he would have to go downstairs and get the key. "Oh, don't bother," said the officer, and passed on. A blind eye?

Some parishioners of St. Ouen remember an anxious moment when a German soldier came to the door and asked about radios. To their astonishment he explained that he was fed up with propaganda and wanted to listen to some real news. He showed photographs of his family, and broke down when he said he didn't know whether they were dead or alive. When he saw them using only one earpiece, he asked why. They explained that they had no more. He left. Some days later a dozen pairs of headphones mysteriously appeared.

The same month Sinel reported that the Germans had instituted a new one-way traffic system in St. Helier, and that for a time road users, mainly cyclists, suffered confusion. The German Military Police, *(Feldgendarmerie)* were particularly on the alert, looking for offenders. These men, who wore a chain round the neck, were dubbed 'The Chain Gang' by the locals. Audrey Lock and her school friends used to call them 'The Dog-Collar Men'. She told me:

I was quite frightened of them, because when things got bad for them in the war, then things got bad for us. For example they might make the curfew really early, sometimes as early as six o'clock. In the summer that's really early.

The Germans took over the Girls' College, and we had to move to the Boys' Prep. which was nice. When we came out of school, we used to cycle down the hill. We weren't supposed to cycle two abreast, and they had the Feldgendarmerie waiting at the bottom, and if you were cycling two abreast, they used to stop you and you got fined a couple of marks.

Going home up the hill, passing the Ballantine's house, where the Germans were, I used to go really fast. I was afraid something awful was going to happen to me.

Although I never got caught out after curfew, I did get hit on the head by a bit of shrapnel. I was cycling on the inner road, near First Tower, on the way to school, and the next thing I remember was that I was in a German car with blood pouring all over my face. Apparently they were having some sort of practice and they were supposed to have closed the road. I had a cut head, and they took me home, where I was ministered to by doctors, and Mr. Halliwell sewed me up.

"A Certain Cow"

Although the "farm" at 'Le Clos du Chemin' was clearly flourishing, in one respect ACH, perhaps in following the entrepreneurial skills inherited from his industrialist forebears, overreached himself. It all concerned a certain cow called 'Wheatlands Doreen'. Wishing to ensure a regular supply of milk for the household and take some in addition to the nurses at the Hospital, he, in the company of three friends, Graeme Fairlie, Captain Harry Ballantine of 'Red Lodge', and Charles Read of 'The Hollies' negotiated with their neighbour, farmer J.B. Michel, to purchase, for their exclusive use, three cows. The cows, however, remained on the premises of Mr. Michel. The authorities came to hear of this transaction and did not approve. And so, on Saturday, 30th May the four were summoned before the Royal Court of the Island to defend themselves.

The whole affair bears unmistakable elements of pure farce. The summons issued to ACH in legal French is worth recording for its own sake:

Prévôt de St Pierre. Ajournez à Samedi, le 30e jour de Mai 1942, à comparaître à St Hélier devant la Cohue Royale devant Justice Arthur Clare Halliwell, Ecr., contre le Procureur Général du Roi l'actionnant de se voir condamné subir les peines édictées par l'Article 92 des Règlements passés par les Etats l'an 1939 le 1er jour de Septembre, sous l'empire de l'Ordre en Conseil en date du 25 Août 1939, pour savoir, le 31 Mars 1942, commis une infraction à l'Article 55 desdits Règlements, dans les termes de l'Article 82 d'iceux, de ce que, en déclarant par écrit au Département d'Agriculture des Etats, pour les besoins de l'aliéna (2) de l'Article 6A de certain ordre intitulé "Milk Control (Jersey) Order, 1940", tel qu'il a été amendé par l'Article 2 de certain autre Ordre intitulé "Milk Control (Amendment No.2) (Jersey) Order, 1942", qu'il avait reçu de Monsr. John Buesnel Michel le 31 Mars 1942 certaine vache appelée "Wheatlands Doreen", il a fait une déclaration fausse dans un détail matériel. Et Prévôt recordez.

(Signed) C.W. Duret Aubin. Procureur Général du Roi.

My father, with his fellow conspirators, duly appeared in Court, and the trial was reported in full by the *Evening Post* the same day:

> *Before the Bailiff (A.M. Coutanche Esq) and Jurats Hocquard & Gallichan*
>
> *Arthur Clare Halliwell*

was charged by the Attorney-General with an infraction of the Milk Control (Jersey) Order, 1940, as amended, in that he made a declaration which was to his knowledge incorrect in a material particular, to the effect that he had received a cow, 'Wheatlands Doreen' which he had purchased from Mr. J.B. Michel.

Advocate Le Cornu said he was prepared to admit the facts except in regard to the statement that it was to Mr. Halliwell's knowledge.

The Attorney-General read the declaration made by Mr. Michel showing that the date given by him did not coincide with that given by Mr. Halliwell. This constituted a false declaration in that the cow remained in the personal custody of Mr. Michel.

Continuing, the Attorney-General went on to give details of the recent action against Mr. Michel, saying there were three other actions based on this. By the Order the producer-retailer was compelled to hand over all the milk from his cows with the exception of a certain proportion which could be kept back by the person in whose custody the cows were. The mere purchase of the cow by Mr. Halliwell did not in law afford him the privilege he sought, seeing the animal was kept in the custody of Mr. Michel, who fed it and stabled it. It had been shown by figures supplied by the Department that Mr. Halliwell did not get milk in excess of what he could have obtained otherwise from the dairy. All that had happened was that he had been able to procure milk direct from the cow in the custody of Mr. Michel. There was no doubt there had been a breach of the Order. In the Michel case he had come to the conclusion that there had been a deliberate breach by an intelligent person, and he had to ask himself the same question in regard to Mr. Halliwell. He, (the Attorney-General) concluded that he had acted quite voluntarily, and because he realized he would enjoy an advantage. Looking at the matter broadly, he could see no difference in the offence, for it was evident they had organised a scheme to get around the Order. For these reasons he asked for a similar fine as in the Michel case, i.e. £20 fine with £5 costs.

Advocate Le Cornu, who appeared for the three defendants, (Messrs.Halliwell, Ballantine and Read), the two latter charged with a similar offence, said nothing would induce either of these gentlemen to say they had acted with the full knowledge that they were infringing the Order. How many members of the community, in fact how many members of the Court, knew of the Personal Custody Order? A person living in the Island was supposed to know the Laws of the Island, but no-one actually did.

Continuing, counsel went on to quote from the declaration, and said that everything hung on the word 'receive.' One could receive a parcel or a dead duck, but could one 'receive' a cow. It seemed to him that if the declaration had stated 'I declare that I have personal custody of the cow' it would have been totally different. Apart from this unfortunate misunderstanding they had not acted as malefactors or infringers of the Order. As a matter of fact there had been no loss of milk to the community; this had been shown by the testing on Mr. Michel's property. The only thing his client benefited by was that he got better milk direct from the farm. He therefore moved for a reduction of the fine asked for.

The Court decided to hear the other cases before giving a ruling.

Despite a valiant defence by Advocates Giffard and Le Cornu, when the Court retired to consider the cases and returned, the Bailiff announced that the Attorney-General's conclusions were granted and the proposed fines were imposed on all four defendants. When one considers that ACH's fee for an appendicectomy was twenty guineas, it will be seen that this was a not inconsiderable fine.

One scheme, however, did work. My father arranged with Charles Read, to whom he paid the cash, and who had an account in Canada with the Bank of Montreal, to send ten pounds in cash monthly to my mother in Curry Rivel. Every month these registered envelopes used to arrive from the Bank of Montreal in London, and we all wondered who our Canadian benefactor was. Little did we know what was going on.

The summer of 1942 was clearly a very difficult time for my father. In June he wrote that he was still finding it difficult to concentrate on his work, but was trying hard. He had had hopes of them spending the summer together, adding "but we must have patience a little longer. Time stands still here." My mother wrote of an old friend, Joyce Milner-Barry, who was now living nearby and was cheering her up. My father replied: "Glad you have found a friend, she used to be amusing."

Amusing she certainly must have been, as this extract from a letter from my grandfather, written to me at the time, shows:

I had a very nice birthday - in the evening your mother, Mrs. Taylor [Joyce's former married name] and Cecil Hunt came to supper, I cooked the meal and the party didn't break up until after 1 am! I didn't feel much inclined for work the next day, as you may imagine!

In July my father wrote: "The summer drags on and am becoming very impatient, but still hope to see you soon." The same month my mother wrote saying: "Hope the Eccles family will be living with you soon. Michael an expert in their idiosyncrasies. But hope he stops there." I had just moved to my public school and was a member of the school Officers' Training Corps, learning the skills of drill, weapons training and map reading. The decoding of this message may therefore read: "Hope the British army will soon be liberating you. Michael becoming an expert in military matters, but hope he doesn't have to fight in this war." My father replied: "They called here last week but I missed them. Michael would be, but I can give him points with other children." Possible translation: "There was a raid here last week, but I did not see it. Michael would be, but I am fairly conversant with German military matters."

June is birthday month in the family, of Daphne and Richard, and our parents' wedding anniversary. My mother wrote: "Busy making birthday cakes and dreaming of our future anniversaries… Love and thoughts always. Dorothea." The following month she reported that "Daphne's first term school thoroughly successful. Christopher [her brother] engaged to be married. The boys done harvesting." My father replied: "Very relieved. Good for Christopher. Be kind to her. My love, Arthur."

By now Christopher Goode was commissioned a 2nd Lieutenant and was married in Curry Rivel to his wife, Wendy Catley.

Peggy's Fortunes Change

Readers will remember the case of my father's patient, Peggy Boléat, who had tuberculosis and was lying in plaster in Overdale Isolation Hospital. In the summer of 1942 there were changes in Peggy's fortunes. She explains:

Mr. Halliwell had been to visit me. He examined the plaster and said it was now useless. I needed a new one and, while at the General Hospital, would have an X-ray. It was well over three months since I had last seen Mr. Halliwell, and then to be told that I was virtually wasting my time lying in an ineffective plaster cast was just too much. I said as much and told him that I had been very badly treated - to the extent that my recovery might be delayed, and if it was not important to anyone else, it certainly was important to me. Sister, who was accompanying Mr. Halliwell didn't intervene. I was too angry to take in Mr. Halliwell's replies. Whatever he said would have been inadequate. So much time, I thought, so much wasted time. As doctors and particularly surgeons were then treated with the greatest respect, I thought there might be some repercussions from my outburst. But no. I had surprised myself with my vehemence. I may have surprised them all.

My new plaster was uncomfortable. Sister found nothing wrong with it and quoted one or two patients who had taken time to get used to their plasters. Mr. Halliwell came to see me. We got on very well and we spoke about serious matters. My X-rays, he said were worse than useless due to the poor quality of the German film. It was arranged that I should go to the General Hospital for a new plaster, and would then have more X-rays next January.

A week later Peggy was back in the little ward. She was taken to theatre and could not believe her eyes:

There, lying on a table, in all its glory, was a box of new Celona bandages, each in a cellophane wrapping. These were the plaster bandages I had been told about, light and quick drying. I think Mr. Halliwell reckoned that I qualified for a present from his hidden store. It could not have been otherwise.

The plaster produced no problems. She could even turn on her side, which she did on occasions, one leg stuck up in the air, as an indication of victory.

Averell Darling recognised that ACH's "old fashioned" attitudes were not always in the best interests of patient-doctor relationships:

Having examined a patient he would say: 'Well, I'll bring you in on Tuesday and operate on you on Thursday,' and the patient still didn't know what was wrong. Arthur Halliwell wouldn't tell them; it wasn't done at St. Thomas's. He would write a letter to their doctor, that was the proper channel. Then the patient would already be on their way out, having said 'No'. So one of us would go out, get hold of the patient and tell them what was wrong, because we had been there at the examination. Then the patient would come back and say that they had changed their mind and would come in.

"Wanton Words"

Despite the trauma of hospital life under occupation there was plenty of humour about; in which the Irish were prominent. I am grateful to Mrs. Vera Hansford, (née Le Maistre) for showing me this poem, which is an amusing account of a day on the Male Floor in the Hospital, called 'Male Flat'. The author, Ray Biggin, was one of a number of conscientious objectors, disparagingly called "conchies", who came to the Island at the outbreak of war; and many of whom worked in the potato harvest. These thumbnail sketches by Betty Thurban are a precious snapshot of Hospital life and its various characters.

Dramatis Personae

Mr. Halliwell	Surgeons were held in much awe. On his rounds ACH was remembered for his nervous manner and a kindly smile.
Miss Carter	Matron was also held in much awe. She was accompanied by a large Pekinese and was renowned for her fierce manner -'you could be torn apart'.
Ray Biggin	Came to the Island early in the war as an objector.
Terry	Also came as a conscientious objector. After the war worked in island television.
Nurse Le Maistre	Margaret Le Maistre came from the well known Grouville family of Les Prés Manor. A much loved person known for her great sense of humour. Her son became a local General Practitioner.
Nurse Mines	Josie, an acting sister, typically Irish, known for her dark hair and blue eyes.
The 'Bailhache Report'	
	Miriam Bailhache was acting as nurse in charge, with the night sister above her. The report was the night nurse's report.
Willie	A male orderly.
Nurse Fanning	Remembered as 'a lovely Irish lady, jovial and full of fun'.
Nurse Walkey	A quiet, precise and devout person, who seemed to flit round like a butterfly.
Nurse Wratten	Joan Wratten was the only child of elderly parents, precise and 'old fashioned' in her manner.
'Pop' Hamon	Charlie Hamon was Head Porter, a quiet man, who was 'always smiling'.
Sister Davey	Was Home Sister, responsible for the care of the nursing staff. Remembered for her frilly caps tied with a bow under her chin. An 'old fashioned' and severe person, also capable of 'tearing apart' recalcitrant nurses.

St. John's Man	Alone among uniformed organisations, the Order of St. John was allowed to continue operating in the Island. Its German counterpart, the *'Johanniterorden'*, was well known to the occupiers. Men and women of St. John's helped on the wards.
Friend Dudley	Terence Dudley, another male nurse, was active in local amateur dramatics and later in national television.

The expression *"war"* and *"the weather"* in one verse is an oblique reference to the custom of handing round news items which had been secretly typed out by those listening to the BBC on their hidden radios. Betty Thurban recalls that copies had to be handed in to her and each was inscribed: "Please pass to Nurse Le Corre" - dangerous, but she was never caught. Later, however, the Hospital Chaplain Clifford Cohu was to land himself in serious trouble for the blatant way in which he shouted out the news round the wards.

An early cartoon of ACH entitled 'Mr. H. Sympathises'.

Wanton Words re Male Flat

by Ray Biggin

It was **half past seven** on Male Flat,
The night staff was saying farewell,
And looking around at the bathroom
Nurse Le Maistre was not feeling too well.

Nurse Mines was enthroned in the office
Masticating the 'Bailhache Report',
Whilst Willie next door in the kitchen
Was engrossed in a dish-washing sport.

At **eight hours** 'ac emma' on Male Flat
We found work was going ahead
With blankets and sheets - 'mind those corners' -
But only two nurses per bed!

They enlisted the help of young Biggin
Nurse Fanning being abcessed away,
And Willie, with bed-pans and bottles
Was making a marvellous display

Amidst these formal proceedings
Nurse Walpy was flitting around
Wielding thermometers gaily -
Young Bernard was feeling his ground.

It was **nine o'clock** on Male Flat,
The nurses were cleaning the wards,
and Medical had some excitement
When 'Brée versus Wratten' crossed swords.

'Pop' Hamon came up with the porridge,
Consistency - dilute plus plus -
It was easier to pour than to ladle
A jug saved no end of a fuss.

At **ten o'clock** on Male Flat
The first shift went over to lunch
As usual they came back in oddments
Although they went off in a hunch.

THE DRESSINGS WERE NOW IN THE FOREFRONT
WITH BANDAGES, FOMENTS AND PUSS,
THE PATIENTS TALKED 'WAR' AND 'THE WEATHER',
THERE WAS NOTHING ELSE TO DISCUSS.

'TWAS **ELEVEN** A.M. ON MALE FLAT,
EACH WARD HUSHED IN TURN, NOT A SOUND,
- "GOOD MORNING AND HOW ARE YOU FEELING?" -
MR. HALLIWELL MAKING HIS ROUND.

NOW ONLY A HALF HOUR TO DINNER,
WILL THE CUTLERY GO RIGHT AROUND?
PLATES IN THE OVEN FOR WARMING -
THAT'S TWO OF THE MATRON'S WE'VE FOUND.

ZERO HOUR NOW WAS APPROACHING,
(NURSE LE MAISTRE WAS COMING ADRIFT)
DIABOLIC ARM LIFTED - INJECTION -
DINNER'S COMING UP IN THE LIFT.

IT WAS **TWELVE O'CLOCK** ON MALE FLAT,
THE GRAVY WAS LEFT DOWN BELOW,
THERE WAS NOWHERE NEAR ENOUGH PUDDING,
NURSE MINES REFUSED TO SAY "GO."

SISTER DAVY CAME ON AND PASSED JUDGEMENT
AND DESCENDED "À LA CUISINE",
AND THERE, LIKE A RAGING TORNADO
THE MATRON APPEARED ON THE SCENE.

THUS THERE ENSUED A GREAT BATTLE
WITH SPLASHES AND SPITS FROM THE FOUNT;
THE SUBJECTS WERE 'POMP AND POSITION',
THE DINNERS DID NOT SEEM TO COUNT.

AT LAST WE GOT ON WITH THE DINNER,
THE PATIENTS IN IGNORANCE SWEET,
WHEN ASKED BY THE "POWERS EXALTED",
SAID THEY'D HAD QUITE SUFFICIENT TO EAT.

CUPBOARD DOORS IN THE OFFICE WERE OPEN,
THOUGH NO ONE COULD QUITE UNDERSTAND WHY!
FROM THE KITCHEN CAME LOUD SOUNDS OF 'SCRAPING',
IT MUST HAVE BEEN QUITE A NICE PIE.

At ONE, with the beds to be tidied,
Or rather the patients 'strapped down',
The first shift went over to dinner,
While the rest tackled 'Surgical Tour'.

By TWO the patients were settled,
Some were already asleep,
Young Bernard had visions of 'blue eyes'
Although trying hard to count sheep.

Intent on being a beauty
Nurse Mines went off to the store,
She couldn't have one brown patch only
In the place where the uniform tore.

Nurse Wratten got down to some bed baths
She scraped, and she splashed and she scrubbed
- The resulting wet patch on her apron
Did not look as a 'nice nurse's' should.

Bread buttered and eggs were collected,
The milk ladled out with a mug,
There followed a heated discussion
on "milk before tea in the jug!"

At FOUR the teas were now finished,
With second round tea on its way,
Nurse Walkey was cleaning the cupboard,
A self imposed penance each day!

Once more the beds were made pretty
Once more the bottles went out
Varied with just a few bed-pans
Where the patients 'could not do without'.

At FIVE with the soup on the gas stove
Already beginning to heat
It didn't seem so long since tea time
These patients do nothing but eat!

The bathroom floor was a duck pond
There were gurgles of joy from within,
Watched by a cheerful "St. John's man"
Young Malcolm was "learning to swim".

About **6.15** was soup time,
Followed closely by milk, hot or cold
The result of this volume of liquid
Is a story that's never been told.

From **seven until eight** on Male Flat
It was hard to tell just who did what
Twas a hive of relentless activity
No one ever stayed long in one spot.

Nurse Le Maistre reappeared in the bathroom
Where we know that she started the day
Whether she left it quite perfect
Is more than my life's worth to say.

Nurse Walkey was 'speeding' the corridor
Taking, tap, tap, tap, six steps to one
She was getting all hard, hot and bothered
Over something that hadn't been done.

We heard a gay trickle of laughter
From somewhere behind a white screen
And knowing the voice of Nurse Wratten
We dared not encroach on the scene.

Nurse Mines was alone in her office
O'er report book her face bore a frown
But when some bright spark said: "Cup of tea, Nurse?"
All her defences crashed down.

The "St. John's man" removed all the flowers
While Willie cleared all locker tops,
Kay removed food from the lockers
In regard to the next morning's ops

It was **eight** o'clock on Male Flat
Another day drew to its close,
The day staff went off on its haunches
The night staff came in on its toes.

We dared not trespass on Male Flat
As the hours rolled on through the night,
But perhaps when he has a few moments,
Friend Dudley will sit down and write.

The period between seven and eight was "a hive of relentless activity" because the day staff had only one hour to prepare for the rigours of the night. As well as all necessary injections and dressings, sterilisation had to be put in hand in case of a night emergency. At ten o'clock all heating and lighting was cut off, and the night staff were equipped with two candles per ward. In the event of an emergency the Germans would be requested to put on the heating and lighting, and it was remarkable how long the theatre staff spent in clearing up, to keep the heating on!

The Russians

On 13th August Leslie Sinel recorded:

Hundreds of Russians arrive for work in the western part of the Island; they made a pathetic sight, and many of them were mere boys, the majority with no footwear and some with bleeding feet; they were under escort of the Todt Organisation and were very badly treated, being hit with truncheons and other weapons on the slightest pretext.

Two days later he recorded the arrival of more Russians, some women. However, these were not the first foreign workers to arrive in the Island. An expert in Occupation history, Bob Le Sueur, explained to me:

There were already a number of 'forced labourers' at work on the fortifications. They were mainly French and Spanish. Of the French, some were political prisoners and were not paid wages. Others were Algerians and Moroccans. The Spaniards fought on the losing side in the Spanish Civil War, and had crossed over the Pyrenees into France in February and March 1939, when the Spanish Republican Government finally collapsed. They were held in camps in southern France, and the Vichy Government, [the puppet French regime which administered the 'unoccupied' part of France] handed them over as a gift to the German labour organisation. Unlike the 'slave labourers' properly so-called, they were paid for their work.

The Russians and other Slavic peoples were regarded by the Nazis as "Untermenschen" or "sub-humans" and were appallingly treated. Many were prisoners-of-war, but were not accorded the status normally given to such POWs. Soviet soldiers were ordered never to allow themselves to be taken prisoner, and each soldier was instructed to keep one bullet for himself. The Soviets did not recognise the Red Cross, which was responsible for inspecting all prisoner-of-war and internment camps, so the Nazis saw themselves free to treat Russians as they wished. Sinel mentioned the unusual youthfulness of some of the Russians. One young lad, fifteen years old, who was befriended by Islanders, told how he was on his way from school with his friends, carrying his school books, when he saw German army trucks stationed at either end of the street. All able bodied males were being rounded up and put into trucks, taken to a railway station, put on freight cars and brought across Europe. Some of them made a run for it and got away, but he was not so lucky.

Audrey Lock was returning to 'Le Clos du Chemin' from school on her bicycle when she caught her first sight of them:

I can remember a group of us were cycling home from school. We saw twenty or thirty Russians shambling along the road. They were really shambling, they had nothing, no shoes. These Germans were pushing them along very unkindly. I think they took them out to the Five Mile Road at St. Ouen' s.

In a later BBC broadcast, Islanders shared their reminiscences. A procession was observed going along Victoria Avenue:

There were these groups shuffling along, numbering about 40-50. They were shuffling along, dirty and grimy and the overseers hitting them with sticks. The soldiers in the bunkers sat watching and grinning. All of a sudden, one of them, a girl, dropped a bundle of rags. An OT guard jumped back and caught her across the head, and the blood flowed. She screamed and jumped back in the column. An old lady standing by cried out and said 'O my God, where are you?'

A resident of St. John told a similar story:

I was walking along the road towards St. John's Church and I saw a crowd of people looking very dishevelled and downtrodden, and I realised that they were Russians they had imported as slave labour. Beside them was a Prussian looking individual with a whip, and he was beating them on.

A further comment from another observer:

If one of them got near enough to a civilian they would ask you for food. They were so hungry and so badly treated. Irrespective of all the good things that can be said about the occupiers it has to be said that they treated their dogs and horses much better.

Many of the Russians escaped and broke into local houses to steal food. The wire mesh in the larder at 'Le Clos du Chemin' bore the marks of their incursion up till the end of the war. Others presented themselves at the doors of local people, asking for sanctuary.

Dr. McKinstry was active in helping escapees with identity and ration cards, and was also instrumental in organising a series of "safe houses" for escaped Russian prisoners. ACH was one of those in the chain and he held both a Russian and Islanders who had escaped from prison.

It was the policy to move people round very frequently to reduce the risk of discovery. And there was always the risk of denunciation by local people. Several were to go to concentration camps as a result of harbouring escaped prisoners, among them Louisa Gould who died in Ravensbrück, and Harold Le Druillenec, the only Briton to survive Belsen. Although people knew the danger involved, there was a waiting list of people willing to take the chance and help the escapees. Many of the Russians were able to escape the labour camps and integrated themselves into island life.

One such person was Tom, who used to attend the same church as Dr. Darling. His is a remarkable story. Towards the end of the five years, Dr. Darling was resting at Sion in a friend's house following an attack of rheumatic fever, when he had a visit from Tom, and this is what he told him:

Before the war I had been a communist, and following university education, I went to people's homes lecturing against God. If I found homes where there was a Bible, I would send the father of the house to a concentration camp in Siberia where they would remain for three years. In the early days of the war, just outside Moscow, my company had found themselves surrounded in one of the great battles of encirclement when the Germans invaded Russia. I was one of two thousand men surrounded by German guns. We had no ammunition left and the Germans weren't coming in close but just pounding us to death. For the first time in my life I said 'Oh God, if there is a God, save me.' As far as I know I was the only one taken alive.

The Germans shipped me down to the Ukraine and there I escaped and went to live in a little village where I was very content working with the villagers. One day a squad of Germans arrived to take all the Jews to be exterminated and because I came from Russian Turkistan, they said I was a Jew. I told them that I was not a Jew but they would not believe me. We were made to dig a trench and then all the people who had children were made to throw them in and bury them alive. We were then made to line up beside the trench, each person with a gun to their head and the soldiers would shoot each Jew in turn. As they came along the line, I could see that I only had about a minute to live. I prayed again; 'Father if there is a God, save me now.' Just at that moment along came a German doctor who had come to watch the proceedings, he was an ethnologist, and he took one look at me and said 'That man is not a Jew, he has come from'- naming the exact area. The Germans believed him and my story and said, 'You won't escape again', and sent me to Jersey.

In Jersey I escaped and found refuge in a home in St. Mary's with a family called Le Breton at Haut des Buttes. They took me in and there was another farm nearby where I could go if the heat was on.' While I was there they gave me a book to learn English, that book was the Bible which I had never read before. As I read the Bible, I knew that Jesus Christ was alive. After six months of arguing against all the arguments I came face to face with Jesus Christ and became a Christian and put my trust in him.

Dr. Darling met Tom again just before he was returning to Russia. Tom said to him "You will never see me again!" "Nonsense" said Dr. Darling; "Stalin's a different man now." He looked at Dr. Darling and said, "I know Stalin and you don't. When I get back to Russia I will be killed."

Another escapee who was cared for in Dr. McKinstry's series of safe houses, and eventually landed up at 'Le Clos du Chemin', was George Kozloff, who escaped from his camp in October, 1942.

He came to lunch with us one day, while visiting the Island many years later, and told us his story.

George was born in Petrograd in 1920 and lived in the same city renamed Leningrad, then in Anjerka in Siberia, and lastly in Kazan on the Volga. From there he was called up in the Red Army and reached the rank of Lieutenant. On 22nd June 1941 Hitler had made the biggest mistake of his career, and one which was to lead eventually to his downfall. He had launched a massive attack on the Soviet Union. Winston Churchill, whose secret intelligence had given him ample foreknowledge of the German plans, warned the Russian Marshal Stalin of what was in store, but he chose to ignore the advice. When the news of the invasion broke, Churchill offered the Russians all possible assistance.

Three German Army Groups penetrated deep into Russia. Army Group A drove south-east into the Ukraine, Army Group C drove north-east towards Leningrad (now St. Petersburg) and Army Group B due east, drove in a straight line towards Moscow, along the line of the railway running east from Minsk through Smolensk, to the capital. By the end of July the Germans were 400 miles inside Russia, on the edge of Smolensk. About 100 miles to the east lay the town Orsha, strategically situated astride the railway line and the banks of the River Dnieper. During the month of August, Orsha was surrounded, cut off and captured, Smolensk fell, and the Germans were within 200 miles of Moscow. In the battle of Orsha Lieutenant Kozloff was wounded and captured. He was taken back as a prisoner-of-war to Germany. From there he escaped and fled to the West. He got as far as France, where he was recaptured near Chartres. He was brought to Jersey with the labour battalions to work on the fortifications, or, as he put it, "I was again captured near Chartres from where I was happily escorted to Jersey." Bob Le Sueur got to know him well:

George was an unusual character. He had the great fortune to land on the doorstep of Bill and Gwenda Sarre who, seeing a half starved Russian on their doorstep, immediately took him in. He was a very good chess player and used to play chess with Mr. Claude Avarne the surgeon who was one of the Island's very best chess players. But George was not the easiest of house guests. He did not seem to appreciate the danger his hosts were in by having him living with them. A group of people who were in the know used to go down to the swimming pool at Havre des Pas in the lunch hour in the summer. George was frequently there. He was quite a daredevil, he would dive from the top board. German soldiers also used to frequent the pool, and George would mix quite freely with them, telling them that he was French. It only needed one German who spoke fluent French to blow his cover.

Because he was something of a risk, George's hosts kept him on the move. George described his time while in the west of the Island:

Your father and I met on many occasions. We were playing together bridge usually in a house situated between the parishes of St. Peter and St. Lawrence. Other partners in this card game were usually Mr. and Mrs. Wedgewood and Captain Ballantine. It was a lively company. However, I preferred to play chess. I also remember a social meeting in the presence of many doctors and the Dean, with a discourse about Darwin's evolution theory in connection with embryology.

Audrey recalls him staying at 'Le Clos du Chemin':

George slept in Anthony's room, to me he seemed quite a large man, but he didn't speak any English, and shambled around. To me as a child he didn't seem very civilised. They never came to look for him, but he wasn't there for long.

Bob takes up the story:

After George had been round the safe houses offered, because he was such a security risk, a more permanent solution had to be found. He was eventually taken on by Ryan, a builder who owned some empty cottages in St. Helier. George was allowed to go into one, and if the Germans had found him there Ryan would have denied all knowledge of him and claimed he had just broken in. This meant that George had to fend for himself. This did not satisfy him and he joined a black market butcher who had unregistered pigs at Maufant where he remained until the Liberation.

Deportations

On 15th September 1942 a bombshell struck which was to have a profound effect on island life, more profound even than the evacuations of 1940. It came in the following form:

Feldkommandantur 515.   Jersey, den. 15. September 1942.

Bekanntmachung   NOTICE

Auf höhere Anordnung werden folgende britische Staatsangehörige evakuiert und nach Deutschland überführt :

a) Personen, die ihren festen Wohnsitz nicht auf den Kanalinseln haben, z.B. vom Kriegsausbruch dort Ueberraschte.

b) alle nicht auf der Insel geborenen Männer von 16 — 70 Jahren, die englischer Volkszugehörigkeit sind, mit ihren Famftien.

Nähere Weisungen ergehen von der Feldkommandantur 515.

By order of higher authorities the following British Subjects will be evacuated and transferred to Germany :

a) Persons who have their permanent residence not on the Channel Islands for instance, those who have been caught here by the outbreak of the war,

b) all those men not born on the Channel Islands and 16 to 70 years of age who belong o the English people, together with their families.

Detailed instructions will be given by the Feldkommandantur 515.

Der Feldkommandant :

KNACKFUSS, Oberst.

The reason for all this was unknown to many at the time. In fact, in the spring of 1941 the German Foreign Ministry had become aware that Britain had asked that German citizens working in Iran against the Allied cause should be handed over. Hitler was incensed and ordered the Foreign Ministry to carry out reprisals. They therefore assessed the value of the captive population of the Channel Islands as a bargaining counter. Detailed enquiries were carried out by the occupying authorities who reported that about 6,000 persons in the Islands were born in the UK, and of these 12 British-born officials were "indispensable". Hitler ordered that for every German deported from Iran ten "selected Englishmen" must be deported from the Islands to the Pripet Marshes in Russia. The German Foreign Ministry and the *Wehrmacht* were unhappy about the proposals. The internees should not be sent to the Pripet Marshes which were in an operational area and it was undesirable that the USA which, as the protecting power, was representing British interests, should go there. The receipt and dispatch of mail would also cause difficulties. The matter was quietly dropped. It only came to light again in August, 1942 through a well intentioned initiative of the Swiss Government concerning prisoner exchange. Hitler became aware that his original order had never been carried out and despite a report from an enquiry that there was no need to intern anyone in the Channel Islands, and that the population had been thoroughly loyal, ordered its immediate implementation on 12th September.

At 'Le Clos du Chemin' there was considerable concern, as none of those there had been born in the Island. Audrey Goodwin recalls:

When the news of the deportations came there was quite a lot of anxiety in the house. I don't really know why we weren't deported. My mother was saying that if she went she wasn't going to take me, and I was going to stay with friends in St. Helier. To my mind that was worse than going. I didn't want to go anywhere else, I wanted to go where she was.

It seems certain that my father was kept in Jersey because of his essential role in the Island's health service. But doctors were deported, and Dr. Oliver, whose family had also left for the mainland, and who had moved down to 'Le Clos du Chemin' from 'Edgefield' up the road, was deported to Biberach. My father reported this to my mother on 29th October: "Very disappointed. Was hoping to have Christmas dinner together. Gid no longer with me. Very bored by myself." The news did not reach England until 3rd March the following year.

The friends who had congregated round 'Wheatlands Farm' with Marion Michel found themselves broken up when the Read family, who were of Canadian extraction, were summoned for deportation, and left on 29th September. It was a bitterly sad time for them all. Marion remembers giving her friend Wyshe a precious piece of chocolate she had saved up, to eat on the journey. At school the next day she told a friend, only to be rebuked with the comment that she needn't have done that as they were all given a bar of chocolate for the journey. Marion recalls feeling very indignant at her stupidity. After the Reads were deported she had their two bikes:

They were much nicer than my bike and I went through both of those. I also had lots of their clothes - I was very lucky and I had Jennifer Oliver's school overcoat. Eventually even the Reads' tyres wore out and we had hosepipe tyres. They used to fray and I used to take a penknife in my pocket, and every now and then I had to stop and cut a piece off my tyre.

Other children, however, were not so fortunate and there were quite a number who went to school with no socks. Shoes became increasingly short. Occasionally, some were imported from France. Marion remembers cycling a long way, to St. Mary where, it was rumoured, French shoes were available. She entered the shop and placed her docket on the counter. The lady in the shop told her, in a very conspiratorial manner, that she had just had some sandals in from France. To Marion's delight she produced a pair with red uppers and white stripes, which were a great pride and joy. Most of the time, however, they had to make do with locally produced shoes, with leather uppers and wooden soles.

Early in the war the Revd Kenneth Preston, a newly ordained deacon, had arrived as curate at St. Helier Parish Church. He got to know ACH very well and they used to have long discussions. He was puzzled as to why my father found it so hard to accept the Christian faith. He remembers him as someone who took considerable risks to his life and liberty to help other people:

He was absolutely dependable and as tight as a drum. He was someone for whom everyone had the greatest respect. In attitude he was more Christian than any of us and he would certainly get to the kingdom of heaven before I did. What a good person he was and good fun!

Averell Darling used to have long discussions about faith with my father before operations, while they were waiting for the engineer to turn on the heat in the Operating Theatre. He found him very outspoken because of his vulnerability:

He operated on Marcella [Averell's wife] and would not accept anything. For this I bought him a book called 'The Bible as History' by Keller. He was intrigued and said: 'I've read that book, I'm thrilled with it.' He was no longer an atheist. He was a man of the utmost integrity and totally honest. He used to take patients into hospital who could afford to be operated on privately elsewhere. He would say: 'I'm bringing him in here so that I can observe him without any bias. If I am to operate on them I won't get a penny. I am making up my mind with any bias removed.'

Amongst those listed for deportation was the Revd C. Atyeo, and his wife and son. As he was unmarried, and with no dependants, Preston volunteered to go in Atyeo's place. The Dean replied: "It would be very good if you would." Preston told me how "his heart fell" when the offer was accepted. The substitution was agreed with the German authorities, provided that two other persons could be found to make up the number. In the event, they were not found and the deal fell through. The ever resourceful Preston, who was only in deacons' orders and, because of the war had not yet been ordained priest, suggested to the Dean that as no Anglican bishop was available, he might seek priestly ordination from an Old Catholic bishop. However, the Dean demurred. On another occasion, when ex-servicemen in the Island were deported to prisoner-of-war camps on the Continent, Preston offered to go there to minister to them. Dean Le Marinel, who was well known for his dry sense of humour, expressed the view that he didn't think this was the time "to go gadding about on the Continent."

Sinel's *Occupation Diary* gives a vivid impression of the atmosphere created by this order:

The effect of such an Order cannot be described, the evacuation of 1940 paling into insignificance in comparison. It is learned that it is a direct order from Hitler and that speed must be applied in carrying it out.

The Bailiff, Attorney-General and the Constables were summoned; the Germans gave their orders. The Bailiff and Attorney-General made vigorous protests and the Constables [parish 'mayors'] refused to be the ones who would tell people they must be sent away to Germany. Early in the evening and continuing throughout the night cars were rushing around the Island with German and local officials armed with lists of the first people to be sent away. In fact, the whole incident created a great deal of bad feeling, because the local authorities were, quite unfairly, believed to be responsible for deciding who was and who was not to go. when Dr. Oliver returned to the Island at the end of the war, he refused the offer of a handshake from the Constable of St. Peter, saying that he would not shake the hand of the man who had sent him to Germany. In point of fact the Constable had merely prepared a list, as he was ordered to do.

Those chosen had to appear by 4.00 pm the following day at the Weighbridge with food for two days, their clothes, a rug if possible, and as much luggage as they could carry. A trunk with the rest of their clothes was to be prepared for forwarding. Sinel comments: "Words fail to describe the wretched state of the Island at the moment, for those not affected have scores of friends who are; everyone is distressed and there is scarcely a dry eye tonight."

Michael Ginns, who went with his parents to Bad Wurzach, recalls:

The order came out of the blue with no warning whatsoever. A German soldier was going round serving deportation notices on those people unfortunate enough to be chosen. There was no time to get ready for those in the first batch. Notices were served that evening. Some people were even pulled out of bed to receive their orders - and they had to be down at the Weighbridge for two o'clock that afternoon.

The *Stabsartzt*, the senior German Army Medical Officer, was Dr. Bleckwenn, who spoke fluent English, having worked for some years in Edinburgh. He was remembered by Averell Darling, as "a really good and kind man." People with medical conditions who were deemed unfit to travel were exempted from the rule about deportation. Bleckwenn would do his best to find some good reason to have people's names removed from the list on those grounds.

Sinel comments:

The impression is gained, however, that the local German authorities are by no means enamoured of the order and in many cases the person concerned has been allowed to 'get way with it' on some trifling pretext - in fact, some of the German doctors have suggested minor ailments which did not exist, with a view to the 'sufferer' being classed as medically unfit.

The Boléat family was affected by this order. Peggy's father and stepmother, Ruby, and brother were to go. Ruby, who was of Jewish extraction, was a special case; and the two were told they would be separated. Because of her condition Peggy was allowed to stay and the German doctor who had examined Peggy asked to see her father's identity card. He said: "I see that you are sixty years of age." Looking him straight in the eye he went on "Take your identity card to someone, do not do it yourself and have the age changed to 65. I happen to know that men over 65 will not be separated from their wives."

Sinel's entry for the following day continues:

Heartrending scenes were witnessed all over the Island today as friends said good-bye to one another. Many of the Germans themselves expressed their sympathy for those affected by the latest order; it is also felt that the German authorities are not all happy in carrying out their instructions, for they know as well as we do that there is not the slightest excuse. The deportees themselves were magnificent, and England can be proud of them; they sang and joked on their way to the quay, and for all the world seemed to be going on a great picnic. For about two hours previous to the time of assembly a large crowd of sympathetic onlookers gathered… German troops controlled the crowd, being armed with rifles and machine-guns at certain places, but they appeared to be very shamefaced and did not look as cheerful as the people being sent away. At the Weighbridge garage a panel of doctors, three local and three German, examined all doubtful cases, and a number of last-minute exemptions were granted because of ill health or where families included very young children. St. John Ambulance members were there to attend to those in need, and the German sailors were most considerate and sympathetic especially with children and old people.

Michael Ginns recalls that during the period that they were waiting to leave a young German soldier who had a little English came up to him and said:

We're very sorry for what is happening to you. On behalf of my comrades and myself I would like to apologise. It is wrong for war to be made on women and children.

As the vessel drew away from the quay, to show that they were still maintaining a cheerful spirit, the deportees raised cries of "Are we downhearted? No!" and sang patriotic songs such as 'There'll always be an England'. At nine o'clock onlookers on Mount Bingham could hear the singing as the vessel left the Harbour.

In England, that same September while staying with my uncle, Dr. C.C. Halliwell, at Farnham in Surrey, I was taken with an acute appendix and operated on immediately. My mother wrote: "Michael had acute appendix providentially while staying with Cecil. Maybury [B.C. Maybury FRCS, a much respected colleague] operated. Everything straightforward. Michael behaved splendidly." My father replied: "Not surprised, always felt he would lose it sooner or later. Glad it happened there and not at school. Expect you had a bad time." To me he wrote, typically: "Hope you have kept it to show me!"

On 15th October 1942 the Jersey General Hospital suffered a severe loss in the death of Dr. Arnold Ferguson, who, it will be remembered, held the combined posts of Eye Consultant and Ear, Nose and Throat Surgeon. Known as 'Fergie', he was, according to Dr. Osmont, a man who was completely dedicated to his work and did not suffer fools gladly, but had a kindly side to his nature. The Germans requested that he treat their soldiers and it is recorded that he used also to frighten the life out of them and insist they took their place in the queue. The eye work was taken over by a French national, Dr. Drécourt, who had to be licensed at a special sitting of the States.

An interesting example of co-operation between the British and German medical professions can be found in the case of young Sidney Horman. Playing with his friends, he was hit with a catapult stone in one eye. He went to see Dr. Drécourt, who referred him to a German surgeon, who confirmed that nothing could be done to restore his sight.

My father had been involved in ENT work during his time as a registrar at St. Thomas's in the 1920s and agreed to take over Ferguson's work. Osmont recalled that he "carried out this extra demand on his services in the hospital with his usual expertise and cheerfulness." An amusing incident is recorded which reveals ACH's special brand of humour. A visiting General Practitioner asked ACH how he was getting on with his new duties, to which he replied with a serious face that he did not think he was doing his job properly. The GP looked concerned and was about to suggest that he should not continue with this branch of surgery when ACH went on to say that in 1920 a tonsillectomy was only considered successful if you managed to hit the ceiling of the theatre with a spurt of blood from the tonsil bed. He added: "I must be failing in my duty because, so far, I have not hit the ceiling."

On 28th October 1942 a large house just outside St. Helier, 'Les Vaux', was turned into an auxiliary hospital, but it was more like a nursing home. Sisters Kennedy and Jouny were deputed to run it, and Sister Jouny recalls the primitive conditions under which they had to work. "It was very hard, there were no lifts and no porters, and if a patient died we had to carry them downstairs and put them in a wooden shed."

In December, Peggy Boléat recorded that, as ACH had promised, she was taken to the General Hospital for an X-ray. The results were favourable and she was to have a further X-ray in February.

From Curry Rivel, in November, my mother wrote: "Dearest, I wish I could take you see children happily settled three different schools." My father replied: "Perhaps you will soon. Cannot think who is paying."

Gradually, the Germans took over more houses, including the Marriners', and the Fairlies' next door. Our neighbour, Graeme Fairlie, with his wife Beryl, daughters Jean and Ray, and son Alastair, received a summons to quit their house on 23rd October and were given eight days to find alternative accommodation. They found a house in Beaumont, named 'Marshlands' in the

Rue du Craslin, known to the family as 'The Snake Road' from its winding route. They were ordered to move all their worldly belongings, except the blackout for the windows which they were ordered to leave in place. Farmer J.B. Michel, with horse and cart, transported them by a roundabout route, down Old Beaumont Hill as the Mont des Grupieaux, which gave direct access to the houses at the top of the hill, was too steep.

The following month my father was able to convey to my mother that the Fairlies had been evicted and the Germans had moved in next door. He did so by saying: "Fairlies moved into cottage in Beaumont. Daphne's path closed." This referred to the path through the hedge by which Daphne used to visit them.

In Jersey, epidemics were beginning to affect the population. Already in June six cases of diphtheria had been reported from St. Ouen's School. Free vaccination was offered to all children, and buses were laid on to bring them in for inoculation. 7,000 children and 600 adults were vaccinated. On 23rd December 1942 it was reported that the Hospital was closed to visitors because of the outbreak. According to Dr. Lewis it was imported by the German troops. This rapidly used up all their stores of anti-toxin, and then left them defenceless. Notices were put up urging the public to avoid any kind of gathering and places of entertainment. The prohibition lasted until August. Dr. Darling, Nurse Minty and ACH all contracted the disease.

In the course of the year it was established that there were cases of smallpox in France. The health authorities succeeded in obtaining supplies of calf lymph from the Pasteur Institute in Paris and 17,000 Islanders, including almost the whole childhood population, were vaccinated. No cases of smallpox were reported locally.

Dr. McKinstry, as Medical Officer of Health, having heard of a high death rate amongst the Russian workers, expressed his concern that there might be a risk of an epidemic. Dr. Bleckwenn made enquiries and replied to McKinstry that there was nothing to worry about… they were merely dying of starvation. On 31st August Sinel reported that there was an outbreak of typhus amongst the foreign workers. The military ordered the *Organisation Todt* to treat their workers better as an epidemic would be very serious. They converted the Jersey Ladies' College into a hospital for their workers known as *'Lager Hindenburg'*, and thereafter the death rate dropped considerably.

During 1942 it was reported that because of the reduction in rations and unbalanced diet there was an increase in deaths in people over 65 years old, who were particularly hard hit by these deprivations. The birth rate was the lowest on record.

In the course of the year rubber gloves ran out. ACH reported:

Rubber gloves gave out in 1942 and after that period we used our bare hands - rather an uncanny feeling at first and frightening if the case were a perforated appendix. We had sulphonamides and Prontosil in good quantity and this undoubtedly saved us a lot of sepsis. On the whole there was no more sepsis than to-day. Hernias and gastrectomies healed up well. There was a bad spot which we traced to the linen thread used for skin sutures. It was ordinary linen thread from the sewing room which we found difficult to sterilise but once we realised it needed double sterilising our wounds healed perfectly, though I never dared open a knee joint but I frequently did an open reduction of fractures.

Dramatically, on Christmas Eve, the long awaited surgical gloves from England arrived via the Red Cross. "Just in time", said ACH.

Sinel ended his diary for the year commenting that although the Christmas weather was dull, their spirits were not, and that everyone was agreed that this would be the last Christmas under Occupation. But much harder times lay ahead…

The Germans have arrived. Members of the *Luftwaffe* pictured outside the St. Brelade's Bay Hotel in July, 1940. *CIOS Collection*

'Monaco', St. Saviour's Road, home of the Halliwell family until 1935, taken over as his administrative headquarters by *Oberst* (later Major-General) Graf von Schmettow, 'Commander-in-Chief of the British Channel Islands'. *CIOS Collection*

Colleagues but enemies- Major-General Graf von Schmettow: Commander-in-Chief of the Channel Islands 1940-42; Commander of Jersey 1942-43; Commander-in-Chief of the Channel Islands and Commander of the 319 Infantry Division, September, 1943 - 28th February 1945.
Copyright Bundesarchiv. Reproduced by courtesy of the Société Jersiaise Photographic Archive, Jersey

Alexander (later Lord) Coutanche, Bailiff of Jersey, 1935-1961.
By courtesy of the Société Jersiaise Photographic Archive, Jersey

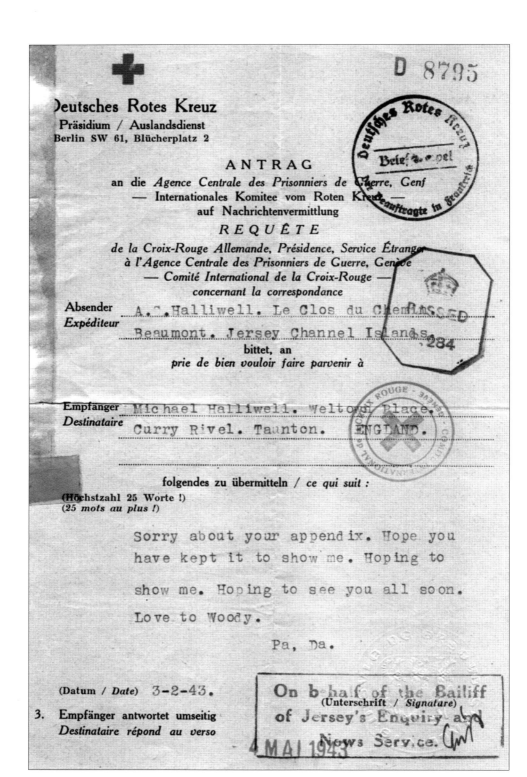

D 8795

Deutsches Rotes Kreuz
Präsidium / Auslandsdienst
Berlin SW 61, Blücherplatz 2

ANTRAG

an die *Agence Centrale des Prisonniers de Guerre, Genf*
— Internationales Komitee vom Roten Kreuz —
auf Nachrichtenvermittlung

REQUÊTE

de la Croix-Rouge Allemande, Présidence, Service Étranger
à l'Agence Centrale des Prisonniers de Guerre, Genève
— *Comité International de la Croix-Rouge —*
concernant la correspondance

Absender A.C.Halliwell. Le Clos du Chemin
Expéditeur Beaumont. Jersey Channel Islands. 284

bittet, an
prie de bien vouloir faire parvenir à

Empfänger Michael Halliwell. Welton Place.
Destinataire Curry Rivel. Taunton. ENGLAND.

folgendes zu übermitteln / *ce qui suit :*
(Höchstzahl 25 Worte !)
(*25 mots au plus !*)

Sorry about your appendix. Hope you
have kept it to show me. Hoping to
show me. Hoping to see you all soon.
Love to Woody.

Pa, Da.

(Datum / *Date*) 3-2-43.

3. **Empfänger antwortet umseitig**
Destinataire répond au verso

On behalf of the Bailiff
(Unterschrift / *Signature*)
of Jersey's Enquiry and
News Service.

4 MAI 1943

Deutsches Rotes Kreuz letter dated 3rd February 1943. Front portion showing my father's message on the subject of my appendix operation.

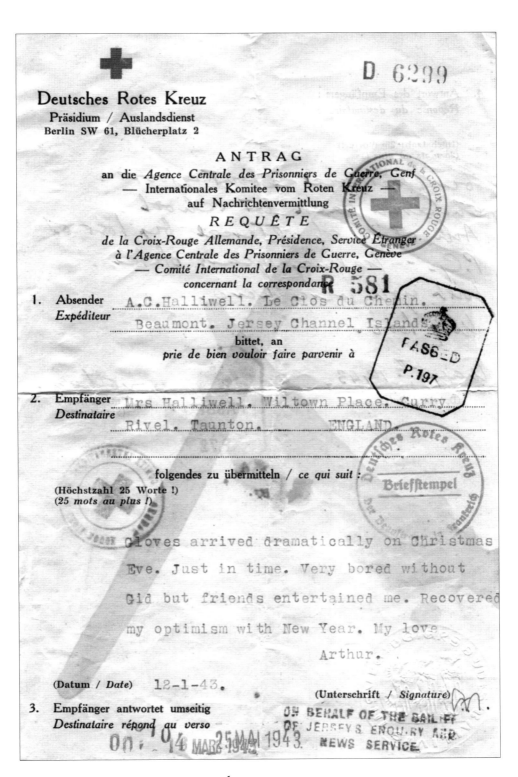

Deutches Rotes Kreuz letter dated 12th January 1943. Front portion showing my father's message to my mother on the subject of surgical gloves.

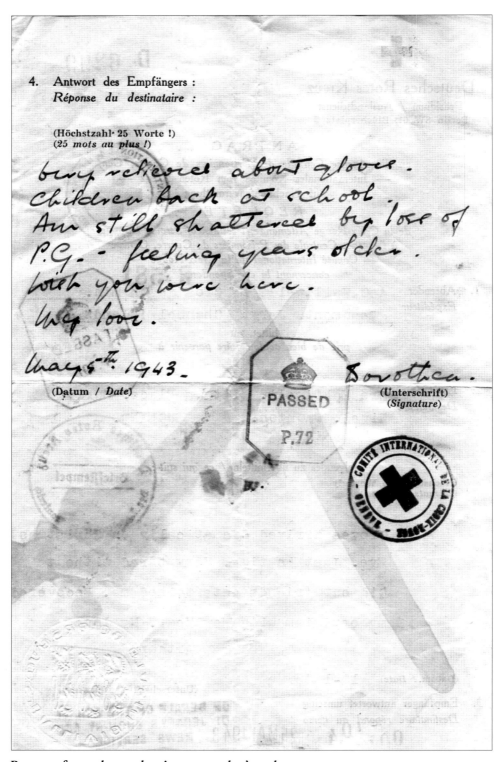

4. Antwort des Empfängers :
   Réponse du destinataire :

(Höchstzahl· 25 Worte !)
(25 mots au plus !)

very relieved about gloves.
children back at school.
Am still shattered by loss of
P.G. – feeling years older.
wish you were here.
Mg love.

May 5th 1943.

(Datum / Date)

PASSED

P.72

Dorothea.

(Unterschrift)
(Signature)

Reverse of same letter, showing my mother's reply.

92

German Land Mine Warning at Saie Harbour.
By courtesy of the Société Jersiaise Photographic Archive, Jersey

Nurse Keane on the front steps of the General Hospital with Dieter. *By courtesy of Gabriel Rosenstock*

Russian forced labourers at L'Etacq Quarry, 1943.
By courtesy of the Société Jersiaise Photographic Archive, Jersey

Deportation scene at the old Railway shed, the Esplanade, September, 1942. *CIOS Collection*

Chapter 9
1943
Disease and Hunger Strike

Leslie Sinel began the year with the news that New Year's Day was rainy and windy, but not cold: "our spirits are bright, however, and we are full of hope." He reported that diphtheria was on the increase and that the hospital clinics at the General Hospital had been closed. He also mentioned that many letters had been received from the deportees in Germany, which were in the main pathetic to read, for all appealed for food and warm clothing, the follow-up trunks not having yet arrived.

As a result of the outbreak of diphtheria, in January Overdale Isolation Hospital was cleared of its non-infectious patients as all available beds were likely to be needed. My father's patient, Peggy Boléat, was moved to 'Les Vaux' to continue her long convalescence.

From February, my father was himself in Overdale Hospital in isolation for five weeks. He wrote on 20th February to my mother: "In Overdale with diphtheria. Now cured. Friends tell me I am having a nice rest, but I never got any fun out of that." A month later he wrote to say that he had just returned from Overdale. He described himself as "bored but well fed" adding, "heavier now than when you last saw me." In April he reported: "Recovered from my dip and hard at work again." But in reality he was not all that well, and his convalescence was to take a lot longer.

The years of separation and deprivation were beginning to tell on him and he was clearly depressed. In mid-June he wrote sadly and only too truly: "Expect Daphne has forgotten me. Richard certainly. Must be dim even for others now." It was hard to imagine the pain of a man cut off in this way from his family, seeing himself fading from the memories of his much loved children as the war dragged on, and being unable to do anything about it. Of course wartime had brought many such separations, but the lot of the Channel Islanders (as indeed of prisoners-of-war) was much worse. In the case of service men and women, there was always the possibility of leave, but we knew there was no hope of a reunion until the very end. I was older than the others, and had more memories on which to fall back. With the camera given me for my twelfth birthday I had taken a number of photographs of him which helped keep his memory alive. Two long years were to follow before we were to meet again with the man who was our father, and to get to know again the man who was partly or totally a stranger.

Like her friend Audrey, Nancy Alexandre remembers how much ACH missed his children: "He was very kind to us, I think because he missed his family terribly, and we somehow took their place. I remember him as a quiet man who did not say an awful lot. When I passed my School Certificate and failed my scripture paper he was very sympathetic, he said it was very difficult."

In the early summer ACH was called upon to perform a difficult operation on a young woman whose hand was badly damaged. Daphne McCann (now Le Marquand) had to help with the hay harvest. Philip Le Cuirot, who was driving the tractor, told me how it all began:

Daphne used to do a lot of work for us, helping with her cob, and so on, and we wanted to repay her. She had a meadow, and we said we would cut it with our machine and tractor. We could have brought the horses, but that kind of grass is hard to cut with horses, you do a better job with a tractor. After what was to happen, I'm glad we didn't bring the horses, I'd never have stopped in time. I borrowed an old truck from my next door neighbour; for petrol we had black market stuff and some we'd stolen from the Germans. I took the tractor in the lorry to Daphne's place at Vermont, Five Oaks. Her father was there, with the Irishman and my brother. We dismantled everything and brought the tractor down. When we got there, Daphne was not in a very good humour, because we'd brought the tractor and not the horses, and she'd have to repay us in petrol. I said: 'Don't worry about that!'

So Philip mounted the tractor, his brother Maurice sat on the mower, and they set off round the field. Daphne told me how her Alsatian dog ran suddenly into the grass. "I was afraid he was going for the blades. I just adored my dog and I didn't want anything to happen to him. So I ran in after him without thinking about getting too close."

But it was Daphne who got too close. Philip explained what happened next:

She slipped on the bar and her right hand fell on to the blade. I heard a scream and stopped immediately. When she got up, my brother had fainted and I had no one to help. I saw the mess she was in, her hand was hanging off, so I took my shirt off and wrapped it around her. Her father said: 'We must get an ambulance', and I said, 'We'll never get an ambulance in time.' The Irishman had disappeared, he just couldn't stand it! So I put her in the front of the lorry and drove like a madman to the hospital.

Daphne remembers:

I sat in the front with Philip, holding my cut hand in the other. I had one artery intact, the other one was cut right through, and all the nerves and tendons and everything else was cut, except a small section. My hand was three quarters hanging off. When I looked at it I thought, there's no hope. I think I was suffering enormously from shock, but I don't remember feeling any pain. I was pouring out blood all the way, up the hospital steps and along the passageway - how they must have cursed me!

When they arrived at the Hospital, the person on duty, doubtless concerned to maintain admission procedures, asked for her milk ration details! She was put in a wheelchair and the flow of blood was stopped. There was a two hour wait before ACH could be contacted, and when he arrived he operated immediately. He spent hours carefully reassembling Daphne's joints, tendons, nerves and the severed artery; and the hand was put in what she thinks must have been his last plaster of Paris. She was given six pints of blood. ACH came to see her after the operation and declared himself very pleased with the results.

For Daphne this was the beginning of a long period of convalescence: "My hand was stiff as a board for months on end. I was told not to use it for a whole year. I went to the physiotherapist and he gradually broke everything down that was stiff. Eventually I was able to get a bit of feeling back into my hand and by the end of the year I was able to use it."

Sixty years later she recalled the "brilliant job" my father did, and today she uses the hand normally all the time, though she must be careful not to hit her wrist because of an exposed nerve. She concluded: "I didn't think they would ever be able to do anything with it. That's why I admire that fabulous father of yours, so much."

The Physiotherapy Department also developed a clever way of alleviating the lot of political prisoners and helping them keep in touch with their families. It all began when a man under treatment for a shoulder problem was arrested and imprisoned by the Germans. Arrangements were made with the Jersey prison authorities for him to be brought back under escort to the Hospital to continue his treatment. The warder (a local man) would sit outside the treatment room and while the man was undergoing treatment inside, his family would be admitted by another door for an unscheduled visit. There was, however, a further problem which taxed the organisational abilities of the department. The man not only wanted to see his wife, but also requested visits from his girlfriend! So the department had to arrange the visits in a way that ensured that the wife and lover did not turn up at the same time. My father realised that this procedure would be a good way of alleviating the lot of other political prisoners. When someone he knew was in trouble with the authorities, he would arrange for him to be diagnosed with some perfectly fictitious condition which necessitated physiotherapy. When the man was sentenced, a request was made for him to be allowed to "continue" his treatment. He would be duly brought over under guard and was then spirited away by the staff for a hot bath (a rarity in those days) and a family reunion. The prison warder was probably aware of what was going on, but as long as he had his man to escort back to prison, he was not unduly worried.

In his next letter, written at the end of July, my father said that his convalescence had been difficult and had taken a long time, but he was "all right now". Doubtless thinking of an incident at 'Les Vaux' involving Peggy Boléat, (which we shall recount later) he subsequently confessed that Dr. McKinstry had said he had been a bad patient, as he could not keep still. My mother replied, on their wedding anniversary: "Thankful you are cured, looking back and forwards today. Glad we are sentimental. Anthony's exam Monday. He will do his utmost. All my love. Dorothea."

This was a sad year for the family in England. On my father's birthday in March, my mother wrote: "Missing you badly on your birthday. Pa seriously ill. Sue and Christopher [her sister and brother] just left. Children and self flourishing. All my love and thoughts. Dorothea." She wrote again: "Pa died April 3rd - I saw him often during his illness this last month. He was happy and comfortable. I missed you terribly." In early May she wrote: "Am still shattered by loss of PG, feeling years older. Wish you were here. My love. Dorothea." And later: "Dearest. All well here. Hope same with you. Very busy and sad. Dealing with PG's belongings. Joyce [Milner-Barry] and other good friends helping me. Your Dorothea." In July she was feeling somewhat better and wrote: "Dearest. Am hoping for more news of you. Spent weekend with McIntyres. Marvellous hospitality. Arranged take you there one day. It did me good." The McIntyres, Ivan and Anne, were a most amusing Irish couple, he a radiographer, who lived in Reigate and were famed throughout the family for their generous hospitality, especially in the realm of wine and spirits.

My father's first reply about PG's health did not reach her until October, such was the time lag between message and reply. "Very sorry about PG. Hope better now." And on receiving the news of his deterioration: "Very sorry darling - was looking forward to seeing him again. We would have had much to talk about. All my love and thoughts. Arthur." Later: "Darling, your earlier letter prepared me. I wish I had been with you. I could have helped you. If hopes be dupes. My love, Arthur." These replies did not reach Dorothea until January the following year.

But there was good news too to share. Anthony had won a Naval Bursary to St. Edward's School, Oxford, and in August my mother wrote: "Woodey joining Michael next term. Awarded Bursary twenty-five pounds annually on your past service. Starting Richard day school till you come."

ACH's reply showed characteristic humour: "Good. Perhaps you can get something for present service. Much more trying. Balance here satisfactory in spite of everything. My love to you all." In reply to her letter about the McIntyres he wrote: "Envy you. Expect you had sherry. Finished Marriner's cellar with Fairlies' help. Had portrait done for you by Blampied. Flattering - strong and silent." Unfortunately, the portrait was not a great success. My mother never liked it and it remained in the loft until it passed to me. I hung it in the Rectory and then took it with me when I retired. Arthur's friend and colleague, Dr. Harold Blampied, also had his portrait done by Edmund Blampied, but when he presented it to his wife after the war, it suffered the same fate!

On 3rd February 1943 the news was received that Stalingrad had fallen to the Russians. At the Hospital one of the German doctors, a Nazi party member who was noted for throwing his weight around, sent an orderly to Dr. Darling, asking to meet him. Darling offered to meet him at a time and place of his choosing. The doctor insisted that Darling make the decision. The doctor turned up at the appointed time, stood in front of him, saluted and said: "Dr. Darling, Germany has lost the war, Stalingrad has fallen. From now on, anything I can do to help, please let me know."

Darling explains:

That was his change of viewpoint. Whether he got hold of Mr. Halliwell and told him, I don't know. I circulated the story, it was worth hearing, because that was two years before the end of the war. And we now had a long way to go, much darker days to deal with.

Cases of venereal disease amongst local girls caused problems. ACH wrote in his report:

The Germans decided that any woman who had spread venereal disease to the troops should be admitted and kept in hospital until they were cured. Any soldier who reported with venereal disease had to give the names of the women with whom he had consorted and the German Field Police would arrest these women and bring them to hospital for admission. This was not regarded in any sense as a punishment but as a form of isolation. It was a good idea because it certainly helped to prevent the spread of the disease. But it had its disadvantages, as on one occasion, owing to a mistaken identity, they brought in the mother of one of our nurses who happened to have the same name as the patient for whom they were looking. On another occasion, the girl who was living with the head of the Gestapo [actually, the Geheimefeldpolizei - Secret Field Police] was found to be suffering with gonorrhoea and she refused to come in. The head of the Gestapo, who inspired fear in the Island, had to call on Dr. Darling and ask him to persuade her to come in for treatment. It amused us all.

In March, arrangements were made for girls previously treated at the Jersey Ladies' College *(Lager Hindenburg)* to be moved to the General Hospital. They were treated in a locked ward in what was the Poor Law area, at the back of the Hospital under the general supervision of Averell Darling. Whilst ACH generally avoided contacts with the Germans, the Medical Officer of Health, Dr. McKinstry, had regular dealings with them, and Dr. Darling had weekly meetings with the German *Stabsartzt*, Dr. Bleckwenn. He was an expert venereologist and skin specialist, Darling describing him as "one of the old school, very well trained, and capable of doing anything." One area where professional collaboration was vital was in the care of these local girls who were infected.

The Germans used to raid the cafes where the girls consorted with the Germans, and as they were a potential danger to the troops they were sent into hospital for examination. They would be kept in for several days for examination and then be seen by Bleckwenn before discharge. Betty Thurban was still a young nurse when she was put in charge of this ward:

I worked on that ward with an assistant nurse who went off ill. I was on my own aged eighteen and that was all! The German doctor used to visit once a week and he had been a consultant in Berlin. I recall him coming up. He was in his late forties. He clicked his heels at me and said he didn't think I would want to shake hands with him because we were on different sides and he respected that. And as he went out of the door, he said to Averell Darling: 'I think she's too young to be up here.' That was really rather nice.

The door was always kept locked and male visitors were never allowed. One day there was a knock on the door and there was a rather tatty German soldier standing there. In very broken English he said that he had permission to visit a girl, and handed me a piece of paper. I didn't speak German and so I was very obtuse and said: 'I don't know what this is' and marched him up to the German ward and got the interpreter. He looked at me and smiled. 'It's a leave pass,' he said. About an hour later I had a repeat performance, so up to the German ward we went. The interpreter looked at me and smiled: 'Another pass', he said. So as I was walking away, I said: 'Would you like to tell them, I might be young, but I'm not stupid!'

Friendship Across the Boundaries

In the middle of all the horrors of the Nazi regime there was one shining light, the German Red Cross. It was strange to receive messages from my father headed *Deutsches Rotes Kreuz*, with an address in Berlin. They seemed like a message from another, saner world which we hoped was in the making. In Jersey the Germans had their own Red Cross nurses who worked in the soldiers' rest homes, the *'Soldatenheime'*, at the St. Brelade's Bay Hotel and the Mayfair Hotel in St. Helier. In his book, *Never to be Forgotten*, Joe Mière recounts how, in June, 1943, when walking up Midvale Road in St. Helier, he was accosted by a young woman whom he described as "a lovely looking young lady" and who asked for help in lifting a box into a car. A couple of days later they met again; she said her name was Erica, and Joe, believing she was a foreign worker, accepted an invitation to go to the cinema with her. The acquaintance rapidly developed into a friendship and a romance. Erica invited Joe to meet her at her billet in Queen's Road.

Erica opened the door and greeted me with a warm and lovely smile. I was really taken aback because she had just come off duty and was wearing a white uniform of a German Red Cross sister. I thought to myself that I must end this relationship very fast, otherwise I could end up as a male Jerrybag and that would never do. Erica then told me that her name was Erica Maria Inga von Kielmannsegg, her uncle was high up in the German army… We started to dance and she got very passionate… I then saw my chance and told her I was very sorry we could not carry on our friendship any longer. I stated that she was a German service woman and I was a very British person and that my family and friends would not understand being under the present war and the times, and with very deep regret we would have to part.

Although Nurse Keane had been allowed to marry a German medical orderly, the same freedom did not apply to German Red Cross sisters, who were forbidden to have relationships with local men. At their final goodbye Erica told Joe that she was being posted back to Germany as she was not allowed to have a relationship with any local man and anyone who was not German. Years later a German friend of Joe found a report about a German hospital train being bombed by the Russians. Among the casualty lists was a Sister von Kielmannsegg, a native of Silesia, born in 1918. She had lost both her legs, and an eye, and her face was very badly burned.

Of course, there were many such wartime romances which came to nothing, but each one bears its own individual pain. Though now happily married to a local girl, Joe still remembers Erica as "my one time sweet enemy." It seems that Erica may have belonged to those many members of the German nobility who detested Hitler but resolved to do all they could for their country and often suffered for their loyalty.

Good News for Peggy

As scheduled, in February, 1943, Peggy went for her final X-ray. She tells of receiving the news:

Two days after having my X-rays Mr. Halliwell came to visit. 'You are cured,' he said, and he added 'You shouldn't have any further trouble for the rest of your life.' I gazed back at him. I could not shout for joy, in fact I felt nothing. It was as if, having waited so long for such wonderful news I could not adjust. I could not say the right words or put the right expression on my face, but inwardly I felt it all and almost wanted to delay realisation of the fact as in opening the wrapping very slowly of a long awaited gift.

At Easter, the plaster was removed. Peggy had to remain in bed for a month. She felt it no hardship now that she had such freedom. After three weeks in bed Peggy was allowed to stand briefly and sit in a chair while her bed was made. After several days of this she decided to try a little more. She took two steps and collapsed. She explains:

Mr. Halliwell was called for. He came and diagnosed a badly strained ankle. He was angry. Matron, in attendance, glowered. Dr. McKinstry who was visiting, came over to us to see what was going on.

ACH, clearly still suffering from the after effects of his diphtheria, fulminated about having to leave the theatre to attend ungrateful patients.

Recalling ACH's five week stay with diphtheria in Overdale. McKinstry turned to him and remarked "Now, when you were a patient at Overdale recently, I don't recall that there was very much discipline up there!" There were smiles all round after that. Peggy's punishment was that she was not allowed to put her foot to the ground for three weeks.

By July, Peggy was still at 'Les Vaux' and longing to be discharged, but Matron reckoned she would be there for some time yet. Her dilemma was solved a few days later by my father's unexpected arrival. Peggy explains:

He had not come especially to see me, but I happened to be on the forecourt as he arrived. He got out of his car and walked over to speak to me. Matron joined him. They stood there smiling at me, and before either of them spoke, I asked Mr. Halliwell 'May, I go home?' 'Can you walk a mile?' 'Yes' (a lie but allowed in the circumstances), 'Then you can go home.'

Peggy goes on to ask a question:

Why should the fact that I had spoken directly to Mr. Halliwell be worth a comment? It was simply not done, and I blushed with discomfort when I did so. Mr. Halliwell and I had, over the months, developed a certain rapport. I felt sure of it, otherwise the strict rule of etiquette would have prevailed and, to my question, 'May I go home?' he would have said 'Let us see what Matron has to say.' I believe that Matron for her own reasons, wanted to keep me at Les Vaux, and but for Mr. Halliwell's unscheduled visit, my immediate future could have been settled without my having any say in the matter. Matron may have wanted to keep an eye on me, or she may have made some kind of promise to my father but, happy with my victory I thought it best not to enquire.

So, after nearly two years and three months in hospital, Peggy packed her bags and left 'Les Vaux' under strict instructions from her surgeon not to ride a bicycle or go dancing. As her parents were in Germany she went to live with friends "for the duration."

By mid-November she could walk several miles with confidence and without effort. However, a friend, Paul, invited her to accompany him to a dance at the St. Helier ballroom, West's. "If you are not allowed to dance" he said, "so neither am I, because I shall be MC for the evening." Peggy explains what happened next:

We arrived early and I watched people arriving. With a kind of dismay I saw Mr. Halliwell arrive with a party and seat themselves almost directly opposite. The band struck up, Paul announced the first number and dancers began to take the floor. I could do nothing but sit and wait, as Mr. Halliwell, his style and elegance remembered, made his way towards me. He came straight to the point, in exactly the same manner as when he had first addressed me in the clinic at the General Hospital two years previously. 'I see it is a fait-accompli' he said, 'in which case you will dance with me.' He led me on to the floor and we danced, sedately and mostly in silence, keeping well away from the other dancers. I had the sick feeling that the whole evening had turned into a disaster and smarted at the unspoken criticism. which was so totally unjust.

She danced with him once more that evening. Peggy concludes:

It was to be my ration, but this time my resentment had flown and it was all pleasure. After all, how many patients celebrate their return to normal life by dancing with their consultant? Did I say normal life? I had made my debut on a very strange stage indeed.

Joint Medical Studies

About July, 1943 the Germans, who always considered Jersey a part of France, attempted to introduce in the Island the 'Service de Travail Obligatoire' by which young men in France, on reaching the age of 18, were conscripted to work for the *Reich*. Large numbers of Frenchmen did in fact go to work for the German war effort in German factories. Large numbers also disappeared to work for the French Resistance.

The Bailiff protested successfully against the extension of this law to Jersey and the order was withdrawn. Local service was, however, expected from Jersey men on reaching their 18th birthday. They were mostly put to work in stores or with the horse transport, which would be difficult to sabotage! ACH and his colleagues did their best to find gainful employment for these young men within the medical services. One such person was Kenneth Podger:

I received my call up papers from the Germans, at 18, so I went to see Dr. McKinstry (the Medical Officer of Health) who had been our family GP for some time. The laboratory had been started by Graham Bentliff's father, it was solely a bacteriological laboratory. We knew him as a man.

I had always been interested in 'the body' so off I went to see Dr. Mac on a Friday evening. He immediately wrote a letter to the Commandant saying that he couldn't possibly dispense with my services, and I started work on the Monday!

It was called 'The States Bacteriology Laboratory'. In those days the island was riddled with all sorts of infectious diseases, which were by far the greatest killers of young people. McKinstry set up Overdale to be an isolation hospital for people with infectious diseases. We were in the hospital complex, but we weren't part of the hospital.

Of course I knew Mr. Halliwell, and my main personal contact with him was in dealing with his patients who were chronically ill due to infection. He often used to pop into the lab and discuss his patients; I so much admired the way he carried on working under those conditions. Apart from our making up experimental vaccines (of which he did not wholly approve) we would be concerned with identifying various conditions. For example with diphtheria there were various types. A number of people became carriers and it rumbled on and on. However ill the person Mr. Halliwell would not just leave them to die, he would always have a go; I admired him so much for that. Some surgeons would not touch a patient if there was a reasonable chance of them dying. They would rather pass them on to someone else, as the death might affect their reputation.

I got the impression that he was a very nervous sort of man, a bit twitchy. Of course he was so thin and wiry and always on the move. I don't think I ever saw him sit down for a conversation. He was always darting around; his brain was obviously on the next three problems as well as the one we were talking about. The only time I ever saw him really relaxed was, funnily enough, after the war, at Kew Gardens when I went down there when I was studying in London. I know he loved his garden.

Peter Falla also remembers being questioned closely about his activities and occupation when he reached eighteen. It was, he explained, important to give a precise answer, for as was generally believed, there was still a distinct risk of young unemployed locals being drafted to Germany to work in factories. So Peter and some of his contemporaries, John Watson, Michael Price, Noël Blackwell, and Frank Killer were invited to come to the Hospital to help out, and to be given training in nursing and medicine as "quasi medical students." They cycled in every weekday, were instructed in general nursing skills, and joined the nurses for lectures by my father in anatomy and physiology. They used to attend Out Patients clinics held by ACH and Dr. John Hanna, and were given further teaching by Dr. Averell Darling on the wards.

Medical students have always been renowned for their ability to hold riotous parties. Frank Killer (who understandably changed his name to Keiller when he qualified) tells of one such party:

Sometime in 1943 we made friends with a Czech who told us that he was a medical student. He was a wild sort of fellow who had been conscripted into the German labour force despite his occupation. He had reasonable freedom to move around and one night after curfew he robbed a German liquor store. There was a sentry at the front of the building, but he got in by making a hole in the roof. He lowered himself down by a rope and liberated a whole crate of Cognac. We celebrated by renting a cottage at St. Brelade's for a long weekend, and the Irish joined us. We had a great party but it was strictly platonic. On Sunday morning we walked with them all the way to St. Aubin so that they could go to Mass. I had a terrible hangover and the only thing I remembered from the night before was passing out from a surfeit of Cognac. I couldn't abide the smell of it for years, never mind drink it.

ACH was always pushing for everyone to have the best training possible. Betty Thurban was just about to take her nursing finals and ACH complained to Matron that she had no experience in the Operating Theatre. Matron immediately sent for her and arranged for her to go into theatre for a few months before her finals. The examination papers were set locally and after the war were validated by the General Nursing Council.

Sister Morgan, who presided over Casualty and Out Patients, proved a good friend to some of the young men whose anti-German activities had landed them in prison. Francis Harris had damaged his eye, and needed to come in regularly to have it looked at. Sister Morgan would invite him into the department, sit him down, take a hot meal out of the steriliser and feed him. For good measure she also gave one to the German guard waiting outside. She also told him that if he was ever in serious trouble, she would let him out through another door and report to the Germans that he had escaped. On one memorable occasion Peter Falla was in Out Patients with her. I so happened that Sister had received some potatoes from a country patient. She had put a few in a kidney dish and placed the dish in the steriliser to cook. ACH came in from next door to put something in the steriliser and opened it to find the potatoes. He was incandescent with rage and gave Sister Morgan a dressing down such as Peter never forgot. History does not relate whether she mended her ways.

The students were also given quite a number of tasks never normally given to medical students, and Peter Falla remembers laying out the bodies of the dead. All subsequently qualified in the medical profession. Peter Falla became a General Practitioner in the Island and John Watson-Farrar took up surgery on the mainland and became a leading UK authority on hip replacement.

On 20th July a letter was sent from the office of the Attorney-General to the Constable of St. Peter, John du Val, summoning my father to attend the following day at 9.30 am at the 'Court of the Field Command 515' in the lower committee room of the Royal Court Building. The reason for this summons is not known, nor the outcome of the interview. A labourer named Dennis Rayson, from 'Brookside', St. Peter's Valley was summoned at the same time. It is not known whether the two cases were connected.

At the end of October, 1943 the Royal Navy carried out a sweep west of the Islands to intercept a merchant ship. They were surprised by the ship's escort and HMS *Charybdis*, the light cruiser, was sunk by two torpedoes. Three quarters of her complement were lost and 29 bodies were washed up in Jersey.

Their funeral service was held on 17th November, conducted by the Dean of Jersey. The Germans provided a firing party and a guard of honour. The coffins were covered with white ensigns, and official wreaths were laid by the States, Parish, Red Cross, British Legion, Navy League, and the *Kriegesmarine* and the *Wehrmacht*. Many local people came to lay wreaths and Audrey Goodwin remembers how she and her classmates from the Jersey Ladies' College used to take turns to look after the flowers on these graves in the cemetery in the Howard Davis Park.

A Courteous Enemy

During the year Baron von Aufsess published a magnificent book of photographs of the Islands entitled *Ein Bilderbogen von den Kanalinseln*, all of the photographs being taken by himself personally, and accompanied by eleven pages of text explaining the history, culture and peculiarities of the Islands. It so happened that my father was driving along the east coast and, passing Le Hocq, saw a German officer crouching, with camera at the ready, framing the tower with a couple of lilies in a jam jar. The fine photograph which resulted made the front cover of the book. My father obtained two copies of that book, one of which I still have. As a student of German I was immediately impressed by the beautiful descriptive style of his writing.

Many years later, some friends in Bavaria gave me a book of essays on Franconia by someone called von Aufsess. The name did not immediately strike me, but when I began to read it, I realised from the style that this was the same person who had served in the *Feldkommandantur* in Jersey.

In July, 1982 we visited him in his beautiful Bavarian *'Schloß'*. After some initial hesitation, he was most welcoming and spoke freely of his time in Jersey. He confirmed that he had been the photographer that day. The book, he explained, had been produced to encourage the military to appreciate the Islands, and to lift their minds to higher things other than the common concerns of soldiers. He showed us photographs he had taken of his life in Jersey, including some of his horses. He recalled reflecting to Coutanche at the end of the war that, of all the Allied leaders, he was the only one who had been in office at the beginning and at the end of it! He also told me of his concern to see that the natural topography and beauty of the Island were harmed as little as possible, and that its beautiful trees were preserved.

When the question of refreshment came up he produced the largest bottle of Gordon's Gin I have ever seen. Knowing the German police's attention to drink driving we settled for a glass of cider, while the children went for a swim in their pool. He told me of a secret diary he had kept during the Occupation, and said that he was being encouraged to publish it in English. However, he was not really sure he wanted to.

It was, in fact, published in 1985 by Phillimore with the title *The Von Aufsess Occupation Diary*. Von Aufsess writes, with evident pleasure, that the appalling difficulties they all faced were overcome by agreement between the occupying forces and the Island Governments. He concludes his preface, "In these small islands agreement between nations was actually put into practice. And the States of Jersey and Guernsey remained the same as before, a fact surely in itself unique."

It is virtually the only voice, as von Aufsess put it, "from the other side of the hill," and it is a fascinating document. In the following pages, the agonies he went through and the conflict between his sense of honour and his duty to the state, together with some of the ways in which agreements with the States were reached, will be seen.

Before we made our farewells, he said that one of the things that had saddened him most about those years was the fact that quite a lot of Jersey people were accused of collaboration when they had, in fact, not collaborated in any significant way at all. He was, I am sure, thinking of the friends he had made among the owners of Jersey's country houses. It is indeed arguable that these very friendships motivated him to do his best for the Islanders.

Make Do and Mend

As 1943 wore on, at the General Hospital, make do and mend was becoming increasingly the order of the day. Despite the fact that my mother used regularly to order rubber gloves from Allen and Hanbury in London to be sent via the Red Cross to Jersey, the Hospital was getting very short, and materials had to be patched continually. In place of cotton wool compressed paper was used, and all bandages were washed, used and reused. In December, Public Health appealed for mosquito netting, ballet dress fabric and similar material to be used for dressings. Dr. McKinstry reported that the average weight for children was seven pounds below normal, and their height one inch less.

As the war dragged on, people did their best to keep up morale. Audrey recalls: "We felt forgotten, sidelined, and we used to do all we could to remain English." The *Evening Post*, in wishing its readers a happy Christmas added, "Jersey has tried to put on a brave face for Christmas. The town has done its best, but it is difficult to instil the natural cheerfulness of the great Christian festival into a people faced with the ever increasing anxieties of housekeeping on a limited budget, high prices and diminishing supplies, and, to so many of them, their fourth year of parting from loved ones."

However, towards the end of 1943 morale was boosted by the sight of a very large number of Allied aircraft flying high over the Island leaving vapour trails and out of range of the anti-aircraft defences. Sinel reported that on New Year's Eve many dances were held and everyone toasted the New Year in with whatever could still be found in the cupboard.

ACH suggested to his colleagues that a dance be held at the Forum Cinema ballroom for the nurses and their boyfriends or partners. The problem was that the majority of nurses only came off duty at 8 or 8.30 pm, and the curfew was in force from 9 pm. Ray Osmont and the Revd Kenneth Preston were duly dispatched to the Field Commandant's office at College House to ask for passes for everyone to be abroad on the streets on the evening of the dance. They put forward their request to the military clerk who obviously had no intention whatsoever of granting curfew passes for the 120 persons who were expected to be present. In the adjoining office was Baron von Aufsess, and they were ushered in.

Von Aufsess was obviously adept at getting round the regulations and told Osmont that he had heard the conversation and had decided that as the request was for hospital nurses he would agree to issue one curfew pass for the whole party! Osmont concludes:

And so at the end of the dance at midnight we set out in one party of over a hundred through the streets of St. Helier, gradually dropping off folk at their various addresses until the main hospital party reached Gloucester Street. This dance and the midnight crocodile procession through the town was a great success and happy occasion.

ACH wrote to my mother: "Facing up to Christmas. Usual institution festivities and dances. Food alright. My love. Arthur."

The *Evening Post* summed up everyone's sentiments, "Standing today on the threshold of a new year, we gaze with brightened vision upon the days of 1944 which stretch out before us, and hope again springs up in our hearts as we long for the peace which will banish war and restore us to normal living conditions."

Chapter 10
The Hospital Chaplain is Arrested

By its very nature the Christian Church is an international organisation. Despite the Nazi efforts to emasculate the Roman and Protestant Churches within the *Reich*, independent spirits within them managed to oppose Nazi dogmas where they compromised their faith. Many painful battles of conscience were fought by Christians individually and in groups during those dark years.

Priests and pastors serving in the *Wehrmacht*, although in every respect combatants, were permitted when time allowed, to minister to the spiritual needs of the troops. In the nature of things, Roman Catholics, with Latin as still the common liturgical language only needed to attend local services, and a priest in the *Wehrmacht* could easily make his own arrangements.

For centuries the Church of England had cordial relations with the Lutheran and Reformed Churches on the European mainland, and inevitably, when the German forces arrived in the Island, local churches were required for worship. Protestant pastors, requiring German language services, needed to contact local clergy to secure use of their churches. At St. Brelade, where prisoners-of-war from World War One had been buried when they died in the POW camp in St. Ouen's Bay, a German military cemetery was created. For a while the pastor used the parish register, but subsequently they kept their own records.

The Dean was approached for the use of his church from time to time, as was the Revd Frank Killer, Vicar of St. Mark's. When a German officer was seen calling at St. Mark's Vicarage, the vicar's son found himself refused service in a local shop because his father was believed to be collaborating with the enemy. Also, when a Lutheran pastor secretly sought out the Revd Kenneth Preston, deacon and curate at St. Helier, both of them had to be extremely careful. Despite the danger, Preston became friend and confidant to a fellow Christian who was deeply disturbed at the cause and course of the war, and longed to see Hitler defeated.

A key member of the hospital team was the Chaplain. Although he did not share their beliefs in every regard my father always regarded the Chaplain as a colleague and would frequently refer patients to him when he felt that their needs were of a spiritual nature.

On Friday, 12th March 1943 the Hospital was shaken by the news of the arrest of their Chaplain, Canon Clifford Cohu. However, Cohu went out of his way to oppose and annoy the German authorities. A Guernseyman, he had joined the Indian Ecclesiastical Establishment, and was made Canon of Allahabad. He was decommissioned in 1935 and came to live in Jersey two years later. On the death of the Rector of St. Saviour in 1940, he was appointed priest-in-charge, *(ministre desservant)*, and also Hospital Chaplain, and he made an instant impression in Jersey. He was an eccentric who became a real thorn in the side of the German occupiers, defying their edicts by broadcasting illicit news from the BBC while riding down the Parade in St. Helier on his bicycle. In the Hospital, too, he passed on the news at the top of his voice during his ward visits. On one occasion he came into a ward and told everyone that the news was good that day. A patient spoke up: "I'm a German national." Quick as a flash Cohu replied: "Then I'm afraid the news is not very good for you." When challenged about the danger in which he was placing himself he would reply: "God is on my side!"

The *Feldkommandantur* had been unhappy about implementing the order to confiscate radio sets, but once it was in force they could not easily tolerate outright defiance of the law. Cohu was at the end of a chain of information, which began with a radio set in the hands of John Nicolle, a St. Saviour farmer. The parish sexton, Joseph Tierney, received the news from Nicolle, wrote it out and passed it on to Cohu. Tierney was the first of eighteen people to be arrested in this connection.

On the Sunday morning as Kenneth Preston was preaching in St. Helier Church he was amazed to notice a former member of his youth group, Dulcie Hibbs, in church accompanied by her lover, the infamous Heinz Carl Wölfle, *Hauptwachtmeister* (a rank equivalent to sergeant), who was second-in-command at the *Geheimefeldpolizei*. The following Thursday the Secret Field Police searched Cohu's room and summoned him to their headquarters for questioning. They put no physical pressure on him, but used plenty of psychological methods, with threats and menaces; on the basis of "We're only trying to help you, if you help us, we'll help you."

Those taken into police custody were questioned at 'Silvertide', Havre des Pas. Donald Journeaux, in *Raise the White Flag*, describes what happened:

A man in uniform, wearing dark glasses, placed me at a table, facing a dazzling light, and I could feel the heat behind me. He seated himself by a window and proceeded to tell me I must speak the truth. He asked me if I knew Mrs. Nicolle. I said that I did and that she was my mother-in-law's maid. Then he asked me: 'What about the news she brings every day, written on a piece of paper in pencil?' I denied any knowledge of this and said that we had never received any news at any time from anyone, whereupon the tone of his voice changed and he became more severe. He said that within an hour I would know what a mistake I had made... He was used to being the inquisitor and continued in harsher vein, repeating the same questions and adding, with much venom, 'You will see! You will see!' I must say that with both the heat and the strong light I was feeling far from comfortable, but I did not think I had shown any disquiet over his questioning... After more delay, he said that if I did not tell him the truth I would be sent to prison and court-martialled and that within four days I would be sent to a concentration camp for two years.

Eventually, realising that another of the accused had revealed that he had received news from Mrs. Nicolle, Donald signed a statement admitting this, but emphasising that he had not passed it on. He was taken to prison.

The law draughtsman, Lisle Bois, warned two other clergy, Dean Matthew Le Marinel and Kenneth Preston, who were also involved. The trial opened on 9th April and, unusually, a Jersey advocate, Kenneth Valpy was allowed to act as defence counsel. However, guilt was assumed from the outset, and all Valpy could do was to plead in mitigation. Jack Nicolle was sentenced to three years' imprisonment, Joe Tierney to two, and Cohu was sentenced to eighteen months. All three had to serve their sentences on the Continent. None returned; they all died of starvation and overwork in German captivity. Fourteen others were sentenced to short sentences, to be served locally.

Paul Sanders, in his book, *The Ultimate Sacrifice*, explains what happened to Canon Cohu next. He left the Island on 13th July for Fort d'Hauteville near Dijon, which was a central collecting point for all those selected to serve their sentences in Germany. From there he was sent to Saarbrücken prison and on to Frankfurt-Preungesheim which he reached in January, 1944.

Conditions there were severe, but up to the D-Day landings he could communicate with his family in Jersey. In his letters home he tells something of the hardships he was enduring, particularly the cold and constant hunger. He was placed in solitary confinement and had to spend his time working ten and a half hours a day inserting hooks into cardboard frames. The German judges assured Mrs. Cohu that parcels could be sent to him, but in fact they were all confiscated on arrival. He was limited to a weekly bread ration of four and a half pounds and lost over three stone. As no air raid shelters were made available the Allied bombing raids sent waves of terror through the prisoners in their small cells.

Preungesheim was also the place of execution for German and foreign civilians tried by special Nazi courts in the district. A former prisoner recalls that in the beginning they were beheaded with a hatchet opposite the chapel, but later a hall was added and equipped with a guillotine. Executions took place very early in the morning and the decapitations occurred at five minute intervals.

In July the following year the Jersey prisoners were transferred to Naumburg-on-Saale where conditions were even worse. Frank Falla, who survived, recalls in his book, *The Silent War*:

We were not allowed to smoke, talk, hum, sing or smile - it was starkly grim, but at no time were our spirits dampened, our hopes shattered, for we knew and had explicit faith that one day our torturers would be conquered.

Canon Cohu's most heartfelt wishes were to be reunited with his wife and to be allowed to bury the Englishmen who died in prison. Cohu's sentence ended officially on 24th September 1944. In August he made one last appeal to the court of *FK515* in Jersey, and he was technically released from prison on 30th August 1944 on the grounds of suspension of sentence. However, as soon as he was out of the hands of the Reich Ministry of Justice he was taken over by the *Gestapo* who sent him to a 'work education camp' in Zoschen on 13th September. Conditions there were reputedly worse than in most concentration camps. From the moment he arrived Cohu was selected for special treatment, partly at least because he was a priest. He was singled out, abused and beaten by the camp *SS*, one of whom predicted that he would not last a week. A week later the prediction was fulfilled and he died.

Paul Sanders concludes:

When preparing his body, Przemysl Polacek, a Czech prisoner, found a small bible tightly pressed against his breast. Such was Cohu's faith that he had managed to hide this most valuable possession, against all conceivable odds, in defiance of repeated body searches and despite the infernal treatment and state of terminal exhaustion he had been subjected to during his final days. This was the last act of defiance of an extraordinary man, whose body was abused and broken, but whose spirit remained intact.

What is the judgement of history on Canon Cohu? Is he to be counted a martyr for the cause? When I put this question to Canon Preston, his answer was unequivocal: "No, Cohu was very foolish, and asked for trouble. He was very dangerous." A tragedy nevertheless.

Chapter 11
1944
The Long Wait

Sinel opened his diary by reporting on mild weather and "everyone feeling optimistic." In February, an American airman made a forced landing and before being taken prisoner remarked to some locals that "the great show was ready to start."

However, the year began with a move on the part of the Germans which was to have a significant effect on the life of the Islanders. For the defence of his *Reich* Hitler designated twelve *Festungen* or "Fortresses" stretching from Holland to south-west France. These were to be held to the very last and the appointment of Fortress Commanders was in the personal gift of the *Führer*. Jersey, Guernsey and Alderney were included, as they were seen as guarding the approaches to the Channel. Graf von Schmettow was appointed to Guernsey and *Oberst* (Colonel) Heine to Jersey.

On 18th January my father wrote: "Living in hospital again. Darling in Overdale with Dip. Had happy hospital Christmas, usual festivities. Looking forward to spring."

Betty Thurban recalls some of the effects of his coming to live in:

There are two things I remember; especially how he was absolutely appalled at the plight of the night nurses. One, that we never finished in time to have anything hot, so we had to heat up our tomato and potato on top of the steriliser. He thought that this was dreadful. We came on at eight o'clock, so we only had two hours, and we couldn't possibly settle our patients in that time. By about half past nine you had to have as much done as possible so that you could sterilise your instruments for the night. There was no pre-packed material in those days. And we used to stand these pies on the top of the steriliser. He said: 'This is ridiculous, I will organise an oven, and wood as well.' I think he went round all his friends collecting wood. That was the only way we were able to have a hot meal all the night. Not only that, but the electricity went off as well, so we had two candles a night for each ward. If you were busy that was all you had. I have one very vivid memory. About ten o' clock we used to go to the Night Sister for our tray of dangerous drugs for the patients. One night I went down and we had the morphine tablets which had to have water added. I was carrying this tray, walking about like Florence Nightingale with my lamp, and all of a sudden, at the top of a longish corridor there was a bright light and it shone straight down. Because there was no one else but the Germans who had a lamp like that I was furious and I said, 'For goodness' sake, put that bloody light out,' to which a very 'Arthur Halliwell' voice came forward and said; 'Nurse Le Corre, please don't speak like that.' He was laughing like mad. And I said to him: 'What are you doing with that light?' And he said 'Ah, that's my secret weapon.' He was doing his rounds. And then, secondly, he also used to bring in from the garden lots of food for the nurses, which was wonderful.

ACH recalls those nights:

My memories of the wards at night are of the nurses going round with oil lamps (Pixie lamps) doing dressings, taking temperatures, and always cheerful telling the patients the latest news, as in 1944 - 1945 there was plenty to tell and there was always somebody at the hospital to spread it around.

As the war dragged on, nurses' hours of duty had become very long, as Betty Thurban remembers: "We used to work from 7.30 am till 8.00 pm, with two hours in the day off." Night duty was the hardest time and Betty recalls that her luck was to be on during the darkest and coldest months, from January to April each year. "The patients were woken at 6.00 am and given a bowl of water, they endeavoured to help, and sometimes the bowls of water got dropped in the dark, with all the attendant problems. When fuel became short, an emergency in the middle of the night was marvellous, because then the Germans would be asked to switch on the heat and the light. The most popular night duty was Saturday. Most people were paid on a Friday, and any illegal abortions would be performed on a Friday, and if they went wrong the women would come to the Hospital on Saturday to be operated on at night. For this, the heat and light would have to be switched on and the nurses would spend as long as possible clearing up, so as to keep warm."

At the end of February ACH developed scarlet fever, and the Ear, Nose and Throat Department was closed until further notice. He wrote: "Been in Overdale again - Scarlet this time. Expect it will be measles next year. Hope you will be there to send flowers. Very well." By March there were sufficient cases for the Hospital to be closed to visitors. In April he was fully recovered and wrote: "Quite recovered scarlet. Educating myself in history. Trying to understand all this, and getting ready for new world. My love and renewed hopes."

At this time a Children's Benefit Fund was created, which my father was asked to chair; he attended meetings regularly and spent much time collecting funds for poor families. The other members were A.G. Harrison, editor of the *Evening Post*, The Revd Kenneth Preston, Miss Phyllis Haines of Helvetia School, Miss Dorothy Newling, (hospital almoner and pharmacist), and Dr. Averell Darling. However, Dr. Darling's ethical principles were not in tune with the others. There was a proposal to have raffles, to which Darling objected. He said that if this were the case he would have to withdraw from the committee. ACH explained that if one person withdrew this would upset the whole organisation as people would be bound to ask what was going on. Darling explains: "He came back to me and finally said there will be no raffles. He wasn't happy, but he conceded my point of view, which wasn't really a very logical one!"

Sinel mentions the work of the fund:

The Children's Benefit Fund is doing excellent work in purchasing rations for people who cannot afford them, this costing about £70 a week… Where once little or none was ever seen, poverty and distress have taken a grip on a large section of the population; children with inadequate clothing and adults with pinched faces are to be met everywhere. In spite of this, however, a cheerful spirit prevails and all look to the spring for the relief of their misery. A number of Red Cross parcels have been received during the month from friends in German internment camps who have goods to spare.

In December, my mother wrote that she was enquiring about operating gloves, adding: "Don't stint yourself or worry about finance. Legacies sufficient here for some time. Keep cheerful. My love, Dorothea."

ACH replied on 16th April 1944, referring to the New Year dance. This was his last letter, as the Islands were soon to be cut off by the Allied invasion of the Continent in June: "Relieved to hear it. Have saved something. Trying amuse ourselves, staff gave dance for nurses. Good show. My love, Arthur."

ACH was now totally cut off from his family without even the consolation of regular Red Cross letters, and Elise Cathro, sensing that he was obviously very lonely, remembers that during this last year of occupation he used to invite her quite often to have dinner with him. He would also quite often go down to meals at St. James's Vicarage, where her sister was in charge of the cooking.

Early in the year an order was issued by the Germans to the staff of St. Saviour's Hospital demanding a list of all the patients in the mental hospital and of all "cripples", as they were to be moved out of the Island. It was clear that they were destined for concentration camps and there were strong protests by Dr. McKinstry and the Bailiff's Superior Council. Eventually, the senior German Medical Officer, Dr. Bleckwenn, agreed with Dr. McKinstry that to compile such a list was virtually impossible. The order was cancelled, or as it was said, "deferred".

Bleckwenn also approached Darling and said: "Hitler has ordered that the chronic offenders with venereal disease should be removed to Germany; they will go into concentration camps." Darling explains: "I hadn't heard of concentration camps, all I knew of was internment camps. 'Oh,' I said, 'they won't mind going into those camps, they will get Red Cross parcels and letters from home every week.' He just looked at me and said: 'You fool, don't you know that no one who goes into the camps they're going into comes out alive. Not one!'"

Bleckwenn discussed the problem with the Constable of St. Helier, Mr. Cuming, who suggested that, to fool the authorities the ward in the General Hospital would be designated a 'concentration camp' and Darling be placed in charge. Bleckwenn accepted this and reported it to Darling: "If you promise to take charge of them and become their warder, and you have total control over them so that they cannot move or leave without your orders, we'll leave them here." Darling replied: "If, under those conditions they are going to die, they will stay here."

In fact, the girls were very well looked after. They were allowed out every day, played tennis, had tea in people's homes and attended Averell Darling's church on Sundays. All this was done with the agreement of Dr. Bleckwenn.

One day Bleckwenn called on Darling to discuss Christianity. He spent an hour with him and Darling gave him a Moffatt New Testament. Bleckwenn said he was keen to continue the acquaintanceship and that they should get to know each other. Darling explained: "I never took that up. Had I formed a friendship with him, I would immediately have been ostracised by everyone else."

But such a kindly man was to show the extent to which even he had swallowed the Nazi racial doctrines. In conversation he also revealed to Darling that he would have been quite willing to practise euthanasia on mentally deficient patients. When Darling replied that they did no such thing here, Bleckwenn just shrugged his shoulders.

Leslie Sinel begins the entries for June, 1944 with uncanny foresight, saying "This is the month when we expect things to happen. The Germans appear to think so too, for there is an attitude of alertness among them."

On 6th June he writes:

INVASION! From the early hours we guessed something unusual was happening owing to the large number of planes passing over… The Germans have manned all their posts and parked waiting ambulances, lorries, etc. in various parts of the Island. Guards have been doubled outside their billets, Red Cross flags galore placed near hospitals and one peculiar thing is the sight of soldiers wearing Red Cross armlets and equipped with steel helmets and rifles! The Germans immediately took over the telephone service, but in spite of this the news spread with almost unprecedented rapidity, smiling faces indicating that the day had arrived for which we had waited so long. A proclamation was issued by Colonel Heine challenging the population to remain calm and warning of the death penalty for attacks on the German forces.

By 3rd July Sinel was recording that the Americans were now close to the Islands and had resumed the offensive around La Haye du Puits, opposite Rozel. ACH and other Islanders went up to the north coast to watch the progress of the battle, but were disappointed when it passed them by and they were left in their isolation.

On 8th July the residents of 'Le Clos du Chemin' were saddened by the sudden death at the age of 48 of the gardener, Geoffrey Gordon Newbery. His funeral service was held two days later at St. Mark's Church, conducted by the Revd F.W. Killer, and he was buried in the New Cemetery at St. Brelade's Church.

On 20th July a long planned attack on Hitler's life by a group of generals at his Wolf's Lair failed and provoked a wave of arrests, followed by a flood of executions. In Germany Frau von Aufsess was unwise enough to comment: "It's a pity they did not succeed." She was denounced by a neighbour and arrested. The fallout from this momentous event inevitably reached Jersey. At this time Baron von Aufsess began keeping his secret diary which reveals much about him as a strong opponent of Hitler, a convinced Anglophile, and a lover of country life, animals and good literature. On 12th August he wrote:

Sonderführer Hohl spouts propaganda and holds up any objective decision. I sense behind this the conflict which the attempt on Hitler's life has set up in people's minds. Reason and a sense of proportion have become suspect as reactionary. Rational argument no longer applies. The shadow of the gallows hangs over us all, especially the nobility.

He shared his anxieties with Coutanche:

There are four people in the fortress who are under suspicion. One is von Schmettow, one is von Helldorf, one is myself, the other is you. The end is on the way and I have an idea we are going to be eliminated. I should not like you to be under any misapprehension in thinking there is nowhere they can send you because they are preparing a concentration camp in Alderney for you, and a few others like you… We will have an arrangement. It may be very difficult when these things happen, to be very precise, but I will try to keep you posted.

The Attorney-General, Duret Aubin, was taken on one side and given a similar warning.

The Alderney concentration camp *(Lager Sylt)* had been set up a year previously. In March, 1943 the existing camp there was handed over to the *SS* Construction Brigade I. The *SS (Schutzstaffel)* under *Reichsführer* Himmler was quite independent of the German military, and the unit which ran the Alderney camp was from the Death's Head Formation, responsible for all the concentration camps in Germany and abroad. The prisoners were landed in the Island on 3rd and 5th March 1943. Their task was to assist with the construction of fortifications, and at its peak the camp had 3,000 inmates.

St. Malo - German Casualties

By the end of July, 1944 the Americans had occupied Granville and Avranches. On 4th August the BBC announced that St. Malo was cut off. The Germans then addressed the task of evacuating their wounded and some American prisoners from the beleaguered town to Jersey.

The Chief Naval Staff Officer was Dr. August Hartmann. He was very popular with the military and clearly enjoyed his time in Jersey, compared with his former posting in Brest where he was regularly bombed by the RAF. He wrote that the inhabitants of the Channel Islands were very friendly and seldom treated him with hostility. In his diary Baron von Aufsess describes Hartmann as "an attractively informal character." Von Aufsess continues: "At one time he wanted to be an artist or a singer. Now, as a doctor, his sober Swabian virtues of efficiency and uprightness are offset by a Bohemian tendency to drink and loose living. But one can't help liking him, as he is clever enough to strike a balance between these opposing elements of his nature, to work hard, to play hard, and to enjoy each day as it comes."

In June, the hospital ship SS *Huxter* had been lost off St. Malo and the freighter *Bordeaux* was converted as its replacement, painted white with green stripes and red crosses. In the late afternoon of 7th August she sailed for St. Malo with Dr. Hartmann in command, and (against his wishes) two escorting Motor Torpedo Boats. The plan was to arrive off St. Malo under cover of darkness and take the wounded on board in the early morning. As the harbour installations had been destroyed, the task was very difficult. Hartmann reported that they came under artillery fire, but that the aircraft circling at the time did not attack them. The ship returned to Jersey with the wounded the same evening.

In answer to a further call for help the *Bordeaux* sailed again early on 12th August, this time without escort. They planned to sail between the Minquiers reef to provide less of a target for Allied ships, and to come under the protection of the guns of the German garrison still holding out on the islet of Cézembre outside St. Malo. They were intercepted by four American Motor Torpedo Boats, but after an exchange of messages by morse lamp the Americans let them go on their way and made off. Outside St. Malo, Hartmann commandeered a French motor boat and ferried the wounded on to the *Bordeaux*, returning to Jersey without further incident. In these two trips they brought back 527 wounded, of whom 277 were taken to the General Hospital, and the rest to the Jersey Ladies' College and the Merton Hotel which had been converted into makeshift hospitals.

The arrival of American prisoners-of-war in the Island prompted some interesting reflections on the part of Baron von Aufsess. For him it was obviously a matter of honour that they were seen to be capable of coping with the demands on their medical services. That day he wrote:

There are also American prisoners-of-war here. One would like to know more about them. With what convictions did they come over to fight in Europe? At the moment they seem interested only in arrogantly demanding more and better cigarettes and sweetstuffs - commodities which we have long since ceased to enjoy. One man's face has been badly burned by a flamethrower, and he has shots in both shoulders. But the enemy receive the same meticulous nursing as our own wounded from St. Malo.

The scene at the Hospital is described by John Lewis:

Every patient who could conceivably be fit enough, (and many who were not) to be sent to billets or barracks, was discharged and their beds taken by the freshly wounded. In the wards the beds were moved much closer together and Army cots were brought in, but this was still nothing like enough. All the hospital corridors had casualties on mattresses, ground sheets or whatever, lying head to tail. The groaning, shrieking and stench were quite indescribable. The Germans had three surgeons who started working immediately on an impossible task.

Ray Osmont explains what happened next:

During the morning the news was brought to Arthur Halliwell while he was operating. I went along with him to the ward and there we viewed the sight of so many of these seriously wounded, some obviously requiring amputation of limbs. Arthur Halliwell had just previously spoken to the German Resident Surgeon and offered to do what he could to help the wounded (including the Germans), because the surgeon was on his own and it was apparent that he could not cope with so many quickly and deaths were inevitable. The German surgeon turned down ACH's professional offer and indicated that he could cope unaided, which was palpably not true. ACH immediately moved into the ward and managed to make his voice heard over the noise of men in pain and distress, and asked: 'Are there any Allied soldiers here?' Came the response: 'Gee, buddy, an English voice! I thought we were condemned to guttural language for the rest of the war.' There were three American officers there. Right away my father spoke to the German surgeon again and insisted that the two or three American wounded should be entrusted to his care. He would tidy up their wounds and they would then be nursed post-operatively by our nurses. The German was far from keen on this suggestion, and said so - he could deal with everyone! In the event the Germans agreed that ACH's action was the only solution for the Americans, who were coped with right away and stayed with us on our wards for about ten days, before being moved to the Fort Regent Prisoner of War camp.

During their time there they were made welcome by those local people who had contact with them. One of them, Lieutenant Haas, happened to have a birthday. One of the nurses made him a cake, and Peter Falla took it to him on the ward, with the agreement of the German soldier who was guarding him.

The German doctors may well have managed better than was anticipated, for the burial records at the German Military cemetery in St. Brelade only record four deaths at this time. Two of them were obviously from St. Malo, as the units recorded were not those of men in the Island. And in view of the meticulous nature of German record keeping it seems unlikely that records were falsified.

The hospital ship *Bordeaux* was to make one final journey to France. In the afternoon of 1st September she sailed for Cézembre intending to bring back the wounded from the naval battery there. She was not to return. The drama of that day and her ultimate fate are recorded in German signals intercepted at the British decoding centre at Bletchley Park.

The battery commander was seeking permission to surrender under heavy bombardment but was being encouraged by his Naval Commander Channel Islands (Vice-Admiral Hüffmeier) to hold out. At 0936 hours the battery commander was ordered to make a fresh request to the Americans for a cease fire in order to withdraw wounded to the Channel Islands, which he did in the early afternoon. At Cézembre the situation continued to deteriorate and the battery commander intimated he might have a mutiny on his hands. He was told to destroy his heavy weapons, think of home and await orders. At 2000 hours he reported that the Americans had rejected a request to evacuate wounded to Jersey, and at 2130 hours that the hospital ship was under "enemy control." In the face of very stormy weather other rescue ships had to turn back. At 0235 hours the next day the following message was sent from Guernsey:

As the American negotiator rejects the removal of the wounded to Jersey, at about 1000 hours today ask for hospital ship to be allowed to return empty to Jersey. Call attention to the fact that this way of acting is 'unfair' and 'inhuman' as he is trying to take advantage of the distressed condition of the wounded for the purpose of blackmail. By negotiating further time will be gained until tonight.

At 0420 hours Cézembre informed Guernsey that the negotiator had already been there seven times and would only return in the event of a surrender. An hour later Hüffmeier sent a message direct to Admiral Doenitz telling of the garrison's brave stand and asking permission to surrender. Permission was received via Guernsey three hours later. The *Bordeaux* was taken to England where her crew were placed in a prisoner-of-war camp. Both these incidents show how tragic was the effect of the Nazi insistence on preserving national honour, no matter what the cost in human life.

A Roman Catholic Protest

The last Sunday in October that year, the Roman Catholic feast of Christ the King, was the occasion of a particularly courageous act of worship led by a German Roman Catholic Army Chaplain in the Island. The mass that day was divided into four parts, Christ the King: our God, our Sacrifice, our Bread and our Life. The second part of the mass contained the following act of dedication, which was certainly not part of the official Catholic liturgy of the day. Its wording follows the lines of the acts of dedication in which many of the German military were obliged to swear to the *Führer*. The message is clear.

JESUS CHRIST, KING OF KINGS, HEAR THE DEDICATION AND VOW OF OBEDIENCE OF YOUR SOLDIERS. WE SWEAR TO YOU, THE MORE A PROUD AND UNBELIEVING WORLD CALLS AND SHOUTS, WE DO NOT DESIRE THAT THIS WORLD RULES OVER US, THE MORE WE CRY TO YOU:

JESUS CHRIST OUR KING! YOU ALONE SHALL RULE OUR HEARTS AND MINDS.

THE MORE A WORLD WHICH IS FOREIGN TO YOU, DENIES YOU AND YOUR COMMANDMENTS AND DESPISES YOUR ETERNAL LAWS, THE MORE WE CRY TO YOU:

THE MORE A COLD AND HEARTLESS WORLD TEARS DOWN AND TRAMPLES ON YOUR TEACHING, THE LOUDER WE CRY TO YOU:

COME LORD JESUS AND RULE OVER OUR UNBELIEVING, MENDACIOUS WORLD AND MAKE IT A KINGDOM OF TRUTH AND LIFE.

COME LORD JESUS AND RULE OVER OUR GODLESS AND EVIL SEEKING WORLD AND MAKE IT A KINGDOM OF HOLINESS AND GRACE.

COME LORD JESUS AND RULE OVER OUR UNJUST, LOVELESS AND JOYLESS WORLD AND MAKE IT A KINGDOM OF JUSTICE, LOVE AND PEACE.

AND TO YOU, WHO THROUGH THE POWER AT WORK IN YOU CAN DO MUCH MORE THAN WE CAN EITHER DESIRE OR DESERVE, TO YOU KING OF ETERNITY, IMMORTAL, INVISIBLE, ONE ONLY GOD, BE HONOUR, GLORY, PRAISE AND MAJESTY, FOR EVER AND EVER. AMEN

The Mass ended with a powerful prayer of dedication written by Prince Eugen of Savoy.

To anyone who had heard the fanatical screaming of Hitler's speeches and experienced the misery the Nazi party had visited on the German people the message was unmistakable.

Escapes

During the latter part of 1944 a good number of local men made attempts to escape to the neighbouring French coast which was by then in Allied hands. Some made it, others, unfortunately did not and were either drowned, or picked up by the Germans.

In November, my father was involved in helping in the escape of Peter Crill, (later to become Bailiff of Jersey – and who has kindly written the foreword to this book), John Floyd and Roy Mourant. The idea was Peter's and they decided to use his twelve foot sailing dinghy which was being stored, in accordance with current German regulations, at Norman's in Commercial Buildings, St. Helier.

ACH was friendly with the family of Mr. Floyd, Vicar of St James's. It will be recalled that Elise, his daughter, was in charge of the Physiotherapy Department, and ACH was invited to the dances held by the church choir from time to time at the hall opposite the vicarage. He went along with Dr. McKinstry and eventually persuaded Dr. Harold Blampied to come along too. After the dances they used to go over to the vicarage for a chat, and were able to stay late, as they had curfew passes. When Mr. Floyd's son John was planning his escape he offered to take letters to my mother in England, and in return my father who had a car, some petrol and a pass to go into the militarised zone, offered help with transport.

In his book, *Lest We Forget*, Roy Thomas tells how, to prepare the boat for the journey they decided to take it to an empty property at St. Clement. During the lunch hour on Saturday, 14th October a charcoal driven furniture van belonging to the removals firm Noel & Porter arrived at the store and drove to Pontorson Lane, St. Clement. To avoid the main roads they drove down the narrow Blinerie Lane, but met a horse drawn landau driven by a German officer. He was kindness itself and cheerfully backed the horse into the entrance of a nearby field to let them pass.

For the next three weeks a professional craftsman worked on the boat and made a fitting for the outboard motor. This was purchased from a fisherman in Gorey village and brought over by Roy and a friend on a motor cycle. Fuel stolen from an *Organisation Todt* fuel dump was used to test the motor, which was in a good condition.

The sea crossing was planned with meticulous care; local fishermen helped with data about tides, rocks and currents and a friendly German at the Harbour Office provided a weather forecast. John Floyd plotted the movement of the German guards and it was discovered that the minefield that ran from Gorey stopped just short of the planned departure point. It was finally agreed to leave from Bel Air at Fauvic at high tide and the night of Saturday, 11th November was agreed as the most suitable date.

My father had bought from Mr. George Montret of 'La Fosse', St. Peter, a small green Austin 7, J2027, which was more economical in fuel than his pre-war Rover 14. He agreed to transport the outboard motor down to the shore. He first collected Elise from the vicarage, then Roy and the motor from his house in St. Saviour and drove down to the coast with Elise in the back, holding the motor, and Roy in the front complete with kitbag. Elise commented: "If we had been stopped it would have been obvious what we were up to!" John himself cycled down to 'Belfontaine' the seaside house of Duret Aubin, the Attorney-General. Their daughter Carette had done her best to persuade John not to go, for she knew the dangers he faced. Some previous escapees had been shot at, and others had drowned. That night they had their final dinner together not knowing whether they would ever meet again. John and Carette walked down to the selected departure point and my father gave him the letter for my mother, phrased in such a way that if John was caught the letter would not be traceable to its writer. The letter was addressed to the Manager of the Westminster Bank, Langport, Somerset, with a request that he hand it to a customer who had come from Jersey. My father said he thought they had better leave as soon as possible because if the Germans had seen his car there they would be sure to come and investigate. He drove to town, dropped Elise off at the vicarage and returned home.

The night was very dark, and despite the danger from German patrols, some thirty persons lined the sea wall to see the group depart. At five past eight, Peter's boat left, followed by another containing three other escapees. To avoid detection they all rowed for about one and a half hours before starting their engines. All went well until the other boat's engine failed and Peter took them in tow. In the melée the remaining engine failed and both boats had to hoist their sails, and became separated. A further mishap occurred which rendered Peter's compass useless and they had to steer by the wind direction.

However, the weather conditions worsened and they decided to let the boat ride and drift while they tried to get some sleep. They were wet through and miserably sea sick, and passed the night in a semi-frozen state. When dawn came, the sea had abated. Roy got the engine working again, and they soon sited a tower on the horizon, which cheered them up. They all ate a hearty breakfast and when the motor stopped again, had to start rowing. Then they noticed that the tide was taking them away from the coast and realised that in the course of the night they had been carried very near the shore, and that now, with the turn of the tide they were being carried in the opposite direction. However, Roy had one more go at the motor; it started again and kept going. They coasted up and down looking for a suitable landing place and at 1.05 pm on the Sunday afternoon stepped ashore on liberated France.

They had landed near the coastal town of Coutainville and, leaving John in charge of the boat, Peter and Roy went ashore and returned with a number of locals who helped them to beach the boat and make it fast. They were taken to a local inn and given a hot wash and a change into borrowed clothing. The innkeeper gave them a hot meal and they chatted by a blazing fire until the evening. That night the weather broke and the wind became very strong.

After a long night's rest, the next morning they contacted the Americans and were taken by Jeep to Coutainville. After a preliminary interrogation they were taken under armed guard to Cherbourg for further questioning, and then handed over to the RAF commander in charge of the embarkation unit. Peter went back to Coutainville to sell the boat and collect their belongings and they stayed in Cherbourg until the following Wednesday, when they embarked, together with their companions from the other boat with whom they had met up, on the old train ferry *Hampton* for Southampton.

On arrival in England they were interrogated by security who took from them documents and papers, including the letter my father had written to my mother, enclosing some of the special Occupation issue of Jersey stamps for us children.

Towards the end of the month, John Floyd wrote to my mother, introducing himself. It was the first uncensored letter the family had received from the Island since the beginning of the Occupation, and gives a vivid impression of the sense of frustration and hope under which Islanders were living at the time:

You do not know my name. My sister is a masseuse at the General Hospital, St. Helier, Jersey, working under your husband. Mr. Halliwell gave me a letter (I escaped by boat from Jersey on November 11th of this year) to send on to you. It has been confiscated by some wretched officials. I hope that it will reach you eventually.

I am writing to tell you that Mr. Halliwell was quite well when I saw him last at 6 o'clock on the 11th November. Quite well, but very impatiently awaiting release.

I see in today's papers that goods and medical supplies are to be sent to the Channel Islands. They will be more than welcome. I expect Red Cross messages will come back in the ships, a most unsatisfactory means of communication but better than nothing.

I'm waiting to go to S Africa to join the forces over there, so that I shall probably never see Mr. H. Again. Will you please thank him from me for his help in transporting our motor to the coast in his car.

My mother acknowledged the letter by return and three days later John wrote again:

Your husband's letter was confiscated at Southampton together with several photographs of mine, and an extract from a book which happened to be in my wallet. I have since learned that this confiscation business is a routine measure. My papers will be returned in 'due course.' Apparently agitation will not hurry the process at all. So I think we'll just have to be patient. I'm even more concerned than you to get the things back as one photograph happens to be of a particular friend of mine. No, I won't claim more importance than you. You haven't seen Mr. Halliwell for years.

It's very nice being in England in spite of 'April not being here' as wasn't it Browning said? Your rations are terrific. Unlimited bread! 3/4 lbs of chocolate a month and any number of cigarettes. I suppose after a few weeks I'll be feeling I want more. Our escape was quite easy actually but it might have been a bit hot if the Huns had seen us on the beach. They had promised to shoot without challenge anyone seen on the beach after dark. I think you'll find a change in Mr. Halliwell, indeed in everyone in Jersey. After four years or more of occupation we are quite willing to take risks we wouldn't have dreamt of taking before.

I don't know why I'm telling you about myself. I'm sure you're more interested in conditions in Jersey. Mr. Halliwell is still in his house up on the hill. I've never been there and I'm afraid all I know is second-hand. The Germans are in the Fairlies' house. I suppose you knew them. The Ballantines are still at Red Lodge. They seem to be doing quite well on the Black Market. I think Mr. H. does quite well because of his 'country' patients. The farmers are the people to know. They pretend their cows aren't giving much milk and keep back some for themselves and butter. I suppose the same ramp goes on in England. Mr H. is looking very thin, but I don't know how fat he was before the Occupation. Middle-aged men have lost double chins etc. My father (Rev. Floyd St. James Church. I don't know whether you knew him) has lost about 4 stone. To get back to your husband I think he spends most of his leisure time gardening. He has got a specially high eucalyptus tree to show you. The landscape in Jersey has changed considerably. The 5 Mile Rd as been denuded of bungalows. Concrete anti-tank walls have been built in many of the bays.

There is a large power house in St. Peter's Valley just under Red Lodge. It's been built by the Huns and burns coal instead of oil. This is being used by civilians and Germans alike. The boilers are about 50 or 25 years old and the plant continually breaks down. Lots of people have kept wireless sets, in spite of the German order confiscating them all, so we knew the news all the time. You can imagine the smiles on D Day.

I wonder if you remember the Aubins (Attorney-General variety) Carette, daughter, used to come to your children's parties when you lived in St. Saviour's Road. Anyway the photos of mine which have been confiscated are of her. She's twenty now. By the way I hope your boys are all doing well.

Towards the end of December, John had his possessions returned and forwarded the precious letter to my mother. She replied, thanking him and saying that she did indeed remember Carette Aubin, who had attended our children's parties before the war. Her reply reached John on Christmas Eve.

Peter and his companions were then kitted out by the CI Refugee Committee and interviewed at the War Office. Peter went to Exeter College, Oxford to read law on a King Charles Scholarship; one of a number endowed by Charles II in gratitude to the Islanders for their support during his exile.

One day, at St. Edward's School, Oxford, my brother and I were summoned by our housemasters and told that someone from Jersey had arrived in Exeter College and would like to invite us to see him in his rooms. We were given permission to go, and over tea Peter Crill chatted about Jersey matters and his recent escape. Roy Mourant and John Floyd joined the forces, and both eventually returned to Jersey. John Floyd married Carette Aubin, and they live in happy retirement just a few hundred yards from his place of escape.

Channel Islanders were not the only ones to make escape plans. Baron von Aufsess was aware that he was more than usually a marked man. Having heard that his wife was under arrest following the attempt on Hitler's life on 20th July that year, he made contingency plans to escape to France in the event of an order being issued for his arrest. He had had identity documents prepared in his own office as a French labourer and gained the assistance of three locals, two men and a girl. They had a sailing yawl in Gorey harbour and with his help they had fitted it out with two outboard motors and a week's rations. He knew that the officer in charge of the Gorey area would be willing to cover his escape.

Von Aufsess had a good friend in a Roman Catholic priest who was confessor to the naval forces. The priest was on good terms with the naval wireless operators who decoded the messages from Germany. They agreed to see that any concerning von Aufsess should be passed to him first and that any ordering his arrest should be suppressed altogether.

Schoolboy Resistance

Towards the end of 1944, 'Le Clos du Chemin' received a new resident. Young Donald Bell, with some of his friends, among them Richard Weithley and Alastair Fairlie, had decided that they ought to do something for the war effort. They contrived to raid various German stores and armouries, and to steal weapons and uniforms. On one occasion they decided to pack stolen uniforms, with the buttons and badges removed, with various food items in bundles, and throw them over the fence of the *Organisation Todt* camp for forced workers at Goose Green, Beaumont. Richard Weithley, in his book, *So It Was*, gives a full account. Donald explained their ideas to me:

It could be argued that we were nothing but juvenile delinquents. I think not. To be fair, having been overrun by the all-conquering Wehrmacht we perceived it to be our duty to resist. Resistance to be tempered by discretion. Being well aware of the appalling Nazi reprisals in occupied Europe the last thing we wanted was reprisals against innocent civilians. Thus, when we raided the German armoury in Mary Street, we planted an OT forage cap as we left with our rifles. This sowed seeds of mutual mistrust and suspicion between the OT and the Wehrmacht, as we subsequently learned.

In 1936, following a fire at St. Aubin's Station, the Jersey Railways & Tramways line from St. Helier to Corbière had been closed. However, the Germans had relaid the track and extended the network to the quarries on the north coast. At Pont Marquet, St. Brelade, where the main road (La Rue des Mans) from La Haule to Red Houses crosses the railway (walk) a spur track was built up the valley northwards. Donald realised that if he could throw the points in the path of a passing train, he would derail the whole train. This he did, and the engine ended up on its side:

My train derailment at Pont Marquet sowed further mistrust within the OT themselves. I shall never forget the streams of hysterical teutonic invective they hurled at each other through clouds of steam and smoke! As I made my way home across the fields I could still hear them screaming accusations at each other. I nearly wet myself laughing.

However, eventually the *Geheimefeldpolizei* caught up with them and called at Victoria College one morning. Donald had acquired a Mauser rifle, weapons and ammunition, which were found in a search of his house, 'The Brae', at St. Brelade. Donald continues:

Following my arrest by the German Secret Field Police in the Headmaster's study at Victoria College, I was imprisoned in the political wing of the prison. There, with Richard Weithley and Frank Le Pennec, we contrived an escape plan.

Early one evening, in February 1945, before curfew, we put our plan into effect. Things, initially, went well. Having spilled water over a heating pipe, we rang the bell for the guard. He eventually arrived and opened the cell door. We enticed him inside to examine the 'leak'. Pushing him in, we ran out, locking him inside. All Hell was let loose, with the guard shouting 'alarm' at the top of his voice, the call being taken up by German prisoners occupying nearby cells. Running out to the exercise yard, we soon realised that our escape equipment (blanket, ropes and a grapnel) would not reach the top of the external chimney - we had to climb in order to reach the prison roof and wall. Worse, we'd have to climb bare handed through the

Soldatenheim, Mayfair Hotel, St. Saviour's Road. *Copyright Bundesarchiv.*
Reproduced by courtesy of the Société Jersiaise Photographic Archive, Jersey

German soldiers relaxing at the *Soldatenheim*, St. Brelade's Bay Hotel.
By courtesy of the Société Jersiaise Photographic Archive, Jersey

Portrait of Canon Cohu by Edmund Blampied.
Photographed by Robin Briault and reproduced by kind permission of Alan Blampied and the Blampied family

The *Bordeaux* hospital ship en route to St. Malo, 1944.
By courtesy of the Société Jersiaise Photographic Archive, Jersey

Jersey besieged, 1944: following the fall of France, a naval artillery weapon at 'Batterie Lothringen', Noirmont Point awaits the anticipated invasion. *Copyright Bundesarchiv*

ZULASSUNGS-BESCHEINIGUNG.
Autorisation de circulation

Listen-Nr. *2).*
No. d'ordre

Der-Die   **Pkw. Austin 7hp**   Pol. Kennzeichen   **J.2027.**
     (Fahrzeuggattung)   No. d'immatriculation
     (Genre de véhicule)

Motor-Nr.   **-**   Fahrgestell-Nr.   **-**
No. du Moteur   No. du châssis

Anschrift des Fahrzeughalters   **Mr. A. C. Halliwell, Le Clos du Chemin,**
Adresse du détenteur   **Sandybrook. St.Peter.**

ist zur Weiterbenutzung zugelassen.
est admis à circuler.   **Bis zum 30 August 1944.**

Bedingungen—restrictions—

                Pflicht als Praktische Arzt.
                Duties as Medical Practitioner.

            Jersey den **1 Mai 1944.**
                   le

(Stempel)
Feldkommandantur
(Cachet du Commandant du Camp)

     President Dept. of Transport & Communications.

'Zulassungs-Bescheinigung' (Circulation Authorisation) dated 1st May 1944, which was effectively a permit for ACH to drive a car. His comparative freedom of movement on the Island's roads made him an invaluable participant in the "safe house" network for escaped Russians and local activists, and also meant that he could assist with transportation when Peter Crill and his friends made their escape to France later that year.

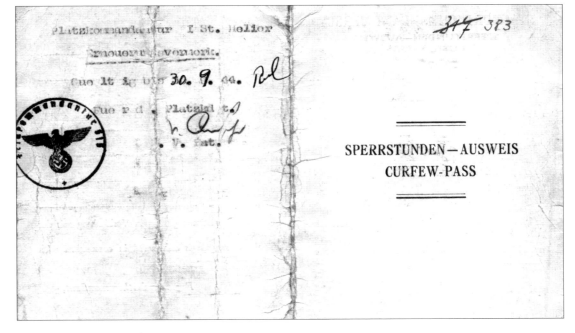

AUSWEIS. Nr. 4

Der Inhaber dieses Ausweises

Mr. Arthur Clare Halliwell

wohnhaft "Le Clos du Chemin" Beaumont, St. Peter

Ident. Karte Nr. 11144

ist berechtigt, im Alarmfalle die Strasse zu betreten,

STANDORTKOMMANDANT.

Jersey, den 22. Aug. 42

Ausweis 'Alarmfalle die Strasse zu Betreten' dated 22nd August 1942. Permit for ACH to be on the streets during alarm periods.

Platzkommandantur I St. Helier

bis 30. 9. 44.

SPERRSTUNDEN—AUSWEIS
CURFEW-PASS

Curfew Pass dated 30th September 1944.

German, civilian and Red Cross officials in the front garden of the Hotel Metropole (administrative headquarters of Graf von Schmettow from 1942) at the time of the first visit of the *Vega* in January, 1945. Baron von Aufsess is to the left of the group. The Bailiff is wearing the trilby in the centre. *CIOS Collection*

January, 1945: German and Red Cross officials at Government House. Baron von Aufsess is on the far left. *CIOS Collection*

The *Vega* in St. Helier Harbour, 1945.
By courtesy of the Société Jersiaise Photographic Archive, Jersey

St. John Ambulance and Red Cross personnel unload the life saving Red Cross supplies at the Harbour, using whatever form of transport is available.
By courtesy of the Société Jersiaise Photographic Archive, Jersey

8th May 1945: the last day of the war in Europe, and the penultimate day of the German Occupation of the Channel Islands. After listening to Churchill's wireless broadcast in the Royal Square crowds pour into Mulcaster Street, towards the Harbour, expecting to see the arrival of the liberation force. However, thanks to Admiral Hüffmeier's intransigence they will have to wait until the following morning. *CIOS Collection*

barbed wire festooning the chimney, which also had broken glass embedded. There could be no going back, so up we went, speeded on our way by pistol shots from the now well-alerted German guards below. Fortunately, in the darkness, all the shots missed us. We eventually, painfully, reached the 30 foot high external wall and jumped into Newgate Street.

In the dark, after an eternity of free fall, the ground came up and hit us, or so it seemed - the impact was so hard! We separated, as planned, my ankles felt pretty wobbly, but intact. Frank departed into the darkness, and I staggered off. Richard was less fortunate, having broken an ankle. He was eventually recaptured and subsequently beaten up, being consoled somewhat however by the kind attentions of a German nurse called Brunhilde.

Donald was more fortunate:

I made my way to the residence of Dr. Mattas, who asked no questions and readily agreed to stitch up my left hand which had been badly gashed by the broken glass. Without anaesthetic this was a bit painful, but necessary. Later, avoiding German patrols, I eventually found a porch in which to spend a somewhat uncomfortable night.

Came the dawn, and I made my way, dishevelled as I was, to the home of my friend Roy Grove. Roy's father, David was a master at Victoria College Prep, his mother, Phyllis, an accomplished musician. Roy and his sister Jennifer completed the family. To their eternal credit and without a moment's hesitation, they offered me shelter, and arranged further medical attention by Dr. McKinstry, the Medical Officer of Health, a stalwart figure in those Occupation days. He also arranged the issue of a ration book, in a fictitious name.

Meanwhile, the German Secret Field Police imprisoned my mother, Yvonne Bell, hoping she would divulge my whereabouts. Fortunately the Grove family withheld the unwelcome news from me, until she had been released. After several weeks with this admirable family it became apparent I'd have to be moved to the country, where I'd be less conspicuous, and at least get some exercise, as I was, of necessity, largely confined to the attic.

My father, Dr. McKinstry and Bill Sarre ran a small network to shelter escapees. Donald explains:

"One evening a car came to the door, (a civilian car, a rarity indeed!), driven by the indomitable Mr. Halliwell. Unobtrusively I got inside, and off we drove. Fortune was on our side, and we reached our destination, 'Le Clos du Chemin', unchallenged by German patrols.

Thus began my second experience of amazing selfless generosity freely given, at considerable personal risk. Mr. Halliwell - ACH, had a dry whimsical sense of humour - I well recall his amused quizzical gaze - we got on together exceptionally well. In addition to Mr. Halliwell, the household comprised Mrs. Newbery [Mrs. Lock], his housekeeper, and her daughter Audrey, a schoolgirl at the Ladies' College. They were all most kind to the new addition to the household. Time passed quickly in such agreeable company and surroundings. Harbouring delusions of artistic ability, I sketched for ACH a copy of Salisbury Cathedral as a symbolic gift. I wonder if this still exists?

Two neighbouring properties were occupied by the Germans, fortunately they expressed no surprise, or interest, in the new boy next door. I remained in 'Le Clos du Chemin' until the Liberation several months later. The Liberation is a happy blur in my memory, so much happiness, at long last it was all over! I returned home to 'The Brae' in St. Brelade much to my mother's relief. For me it was a strange experience, British troops in khaki - now in total, but benevolent control - Germans in field grey, taking their orders meekly, all arrogance gone, and now totally powerless. It was equally strange returning to classes at Victoria College - life had suddenly become very humdrum, and mundane!

On another occasion, Alastair Fairlie, who had lived next door to 'Le Clos du Chemin' until evicted by the Germans, was walking with a friend past his old house, 'Le Grupé', when he noticed some German kit outside the front door. He and Roy Grove ran forward, grabbed the kit and ran off down the field across the road, pursued by pistol shots from the enraged Warrant Officer. Running down towards St. Peter's Valley they reached a fence, Roy scrambled over, but Alastair impaled himself on the barbed wire, and cut his thigh badly. The boys dropped their loot and Alastair went home, with Roy's help, to their temporary home in Beaumont. Seeing the two boys at the door, the formidable Mrs. Fairlie demanded: "What's the meaning of this?" "Alastair's got a cut," said Roy and, ushering his friend in, beat a quick retreat. Alastair was taken in and ACH called to sew up his wound. When his father returned from the office at the end of the day he gave Alastair the biggest hiding of his life. His ardour thus dampened he confined his activities to minor crimes like turning round signposts.

What was the point of all this? Donald expresses his opinion about their escapades:

Fundamentally, we felt we had to do our share to help with the war. And so we did what we could. Whether anything we did had any vestigial effect on the ultimate outcome is very doubtful! In most parts of occupied Europe the Nazis behaved in an appalling fashion. In Jersey we escaped the worst. But had we been caught and imprisoned before D-Day I would almost certainly not be writing this.

On a happier note these jottings give me an opportunity I should have taken many years ago, an opportunity to state that I feel an enormous sense of gratitude to the two families who aided and sheltered me in those troubled Occupation times. The risks taken on my account were beyond all human expectations.

Poverty and Distress

Towards the end of the Occupation drugs ran increasingly short. A local GP, a French national, Dr. Labesse, and his wife, had helped a great deal by getting supplies over from France; and with the help of the Germans some sulphonamides used to come into the Island. However, after the Allied invasion of France and their capture of the neighbouring ports on the French coast, all supplies ceased.

The treatment of diabetics was a particular problem. Dr. McKinstry had little success in getting medication through the Red Cross. When he realised that supplies were running out, he had all the insulin patients brought into hospital where they were kept on a specially controlled diet. One by one they went into a coma and died. One patient, however, survived. Maurice Green discharged himself and lived rough, working out of doors. One day a German soldier who must have heard of his illness gave him some insulin. The man in question had scoured France for insulin for his mother, and found some, only to be told that his mother had been killed in an RAF raid on Hamburg. He arrived weeping at the Greens' house, thrust the insulin into Maurice's hand, and left, still weeping, without giving his name.

Tuberculosis, too, was a serious problem. John Lewis explains:

As might have been expected, the TB germ took full advantage of the conditions, and cases began to multiply rapidly. New drugs like streptomycin had not reached us, and the special rations allocated for TB were not really sufficient to make much difference. Bone tubercle, (which had previously been rare in the Island) made its appearance and had to be treated as best we could with the limited drugs available.

Sadly, Dr. Harold Blampied, who had served with loyalty and dedication as anaesthetist throughout the Occupation, contracted the disease, and, though reunited with his family after the war, survived for only a few years.

Mary Le Sueur remembers a desperate plan for her husband and another person (she never knew who) to escape with a boat to find the Americans, now arrived in St. Malo, and obtain drugs from them. Fortunately, the Red Cross ship bringing food parcels also brought drugs and the plan was shelved.

The X-Ray Department, which had up till then relied on film imported with German co-operation, from Holland, had to conserve supplies, and the department had very little to do. The radiologist, Lorna Mackintosh, found herself called upon to assist in the Maternity Hospital.

As the month of December wore on, Sinel reported a steady reduction in rations, and the electricity supply was cut back. In a bout of severe weather many people had to buy tar to mix with ashes and sawdust: "'tar queues' are always long, and people with all sorts of containers and conveyances have to wait at times for many hours in the pouring rain and bitterly cold weather. Some people have had to cut up blankets with which to make underclothing." At the end of the month the bus services ceased completely owing to the exhaustion of anthracite and charcoal stocks. Sinel ends:

The trials of the Occupation are telling on everyone, and many quite young men have been affected through overstrain caused by the perpetual heavy work which must be undertaken in order to live, mostly the carting and sawing of wood.

Prolonged discussions took place between the Island authorities and the German civil administrators concerning the increasingly desperate food and health situation. Dr. McKinstry produced a report entitled: 'A survey of the effects of the Occupation on the people of Jersey'. In this he wrote:

During the last few weeks the ration has a calorie of 1,500, which, with a few extras, which most people managed to obtain, could be made up to 2,000 and although grossly deficient in fat and protein was sufficient to ward off the major manifestations of starvation.

The extent to which Jersey has suffered is shown by the fall in the height and weight of children, the prevalence of malnutrition amongst the working class in town, the gross deficiency in clothes and footwear, and the increase in the incidence of lice, scabies, ringworm and septic skin diseases largely due to the lack of soap.

During the last few weeks the sugar ration has ceased, we are about to have a milk-less day for adults, the butter is coming to an end and further reductions are in the offing. There is no soap and fuel is only sufficient for communal cooking, and laundries have closed down. The people, frantic for fuel are destroying the shrubs and trees in the neighbourhood of the town. In inclement weather children arrive at school with insufficient clothing and leaking shoes. In the schools there is no heating and no means of drying clothes. Skin troubles are causing serious absenteeism; the milk for schoolchildren has been stopped.

The drug situation is bad, anaesthetics are coming to an end in spite of the most drastic economy. Salicylics, bromides, hypnotic drugs and liver extracts are completely missing.

Poverty and distress have taken a grip on a large section of the population.

Although this situation was desperate, my father did report that no Islander died of starvation, except two people who were unable to fend for themselves.

About this time a young boy, nine years of age, was brought in to the Hospital suffering from an acute appendicitis. It was clear to my father that, if he was not operated on soon, he was going to die. They had no anaesthetics. ACH said to Harold Blampied, who was serving as anaesthetist, "What can we do for this boy? If we don't operate soon, he's bound to die." Harold thought for a while and then replied: "I tell you what, I've got a bottle of brandy which I've been keeping for the Liberation, I could go and get it." As there was a curfew in operation ACH expressed doubts about Harold getting home and back to the Hospital safely without being discovered. Harold agreed to have a try. In due course he returned with the precious bottle. The boy was prepared for the operation and the brandy poured down his throat until he lost consciousness. Nurse Margaret Le Maistre (now Mrs. Perkins) remembers being asked to hold him in case he moved. He moved his arms round a bit, but the operation passed off without incident, he felt nothing, came round in due course and made a complete recovery. He must, however, have had a huge hangover!

Audrey recalls these hard times:

Once the invasion of France took place, the Germans were as cut off as we were. In a way they were worse off. But we got very short of food. I can remember my mother making flour with potatoes, and carrot tea, which was vile, and acorn coffee. I can see her now making it all in the pantry beyond the kitchen. We had rabbits in the yard, and when we were having it to eat, she always used to tell us it was not our rabbit, but someone else's. At times we had no coal, no light, no radio, or anything else. You couldn't buy anything. I grew up from eleven to sixteen with no new clothes. You had hand-me-downs. Nancy O'Neill was a great friend of mine, she used to live in a bungalow at the bottom of the hill. I was very envious of her because her parents had a sports' shop and were friendly with people in De Gruchy's department store. I remember she had a blanket coat made, out of a blue blanket. It was absolutely lovely. I went with her for fittings, because there was nothing in the shops, and you used to have to take your own stuff.

Nancy's parents had taken a good deal of trouble to buy in stocks of food and clothes for their children. Nancy remembers her mother buying a range of shoes of different sizes into which they grew as time went on. With their links with the country they were better off for food than many people in the town.

The deteriorating situation in the Island was discussed at top level by the German High Command, and it was even suggested that the entire civilian population should be evacuated and that Britain would have to find the ships to carry them.

Baron von Aufsess pondered the situation in his diary on 21st August:

We must be guided by three considerations: first our honour as soldiers, second, commonsense, third, humanitarian motives. It is now pretty obvious that the British do not intend to take the islands by force, but to spare them and let them fall into their hands like ripe fruit at the end of the war. If Germany is defeated this year, the safety of the islands is assured. But if the end is further delayed, the British must either take possession of the islands, or do something about supporting the civilian population, unless the islanders are to starve, which one may safely assume would be the last thing the British government would wish.

If the end of the war is to be further delayed, the next urgent task will be to arrange for the Red Cross to bring supplies for the islanders, and they might well at the same time be bringing supplies for the German garrison. As long as the Germans are masters in the islands, it would be hardly expedient to let them starve.

But that is precisely what Churchill intended. On 19th September, Cruickshank records that the German Foreign Ministry asked the protecting power to inform Britain that "on the former British Channel Islands supplies for the civilian population are exhausted." They would allow evacuation of all not of military age, or the sending of food. In Britain there was general agreement about the desirability of sending food. Churchill, however, did not agree. He was in favour of isolating the Islands entirely and endorsed a proposal that the garrison should be starved out, adding in the margin: "Let 'em starve. No fighting. They can rot at their leisure." Though he was not referring specifically to the Islanders, he added on 27th September: "I am entirely opposed to our sending any rations to the Channel Islands ostensibly for the civil population, but in fact enabling the German garrison to prolong their resistance. I therefore prefer to evacuate the women and children at once… It is possible that the Germans would accept this."

Eventually, the British sent to the British Legation in Berne a message informing the Germans that as long as they remained in occupation it was their responsibility to feed the population. If they were not going to do so, food would be sent through the Red Cross.

The discussions went on, both internally in Britain and Germany and between the two governments through the protecting power, and finally, on 7th November, Churchill relented and agreed that food parcels be sent on the understanding that the Germans continued to be responsible for the civilian rations. He also agreed that medical supplies might be sent, although the Germans might take them. This decision was notified to the Germans the same day and the German reply received two weeks later. They agreed to the proposals, they had hitherto cared for all the inhabitants and would continue to do so; they offered safe conduct to Red Cross ships.

Von Aufsess made it clear that he would not support any proposal for the forces to take the population's food to their detriment. Von Aufsess confessed to having spent sleepless nights worrying over the situation, and he wrote on 11th November:

After mulling this over all night, in the morning I called my staff officers together to acquaint them with my assessment of the situation and my determination never to serve as hangman's assistant in the annihilation of the population or lend my name and responsible position as head of civil affairs to any orders to that effect. If such a barbaric measure as depriving the civilian population of all food to enable us to hold out longer should be carried out, I should certainly not be here to witness the final surrender of the islands minus islanders, as I should long since have been dead, as a preferable choice.

At this time von Aufsess received news that his wife had been arrested by the *Gestapo* and was to be brought before the Peoples' Court. He wrote:

It is useless to try to put my feelings into words. I am utterly overcome and shall never have another minute's peace. She, my lovely, sensitive, delicate young wife, immured behind prison bars... That this courageous honest woman should now be arraigned at some monstrous show trial seems to me to belong to the dark days of the French or Russian revolutions and to have nothing to do with the true spirit of the German people.

Islanders' spirits were revived by an announcement by the Bailiff on 8th December:

I am officially informed by the German Military Authorities that a Red Cross ship was weather permitting, due to leave Lisbon on Thursday, December 7th, for the Channel Islands.

A few days later he announced that the German Government had approached the British Government with a view to sending supplies to the Channel Islands. In view of reports received, the British Government had decided that it was right to send additional quantities of medicines, soap and food parcels.

The *Vega* Brings Relief

At last, on New Year's Eve the Red Cross ship *Vega* arrived in St. Helier with the first supply of food parcels for the hungry population. There were two for each civilian, weighing 9lbs, 10 oz, containing usually: 6 ozs of chocolate, 20 biscuits, 4 ozs tea, 20 ozs butter, 6 ozs sugar, 2ozs milk powder, 1lb tin of marmalade, 5 oz tin of sardines, 8 oz tin of raisins, 6 oz tin of prunes, 4 oz tin of cheese, 3 oz tablet of soap, 1 oz pepper and salt.

Medical supplies, too, were sent. At the General Hospital the medical students were given the task of unpacking them and making an inventory of the contents. A German guard was posted to see all went properly and Peter Falla remembers coming upon a message in one of the packages. When the guard was not looking he smuggled it into his pocket. It was a message from one of the packers saying: "Good luck to you. Annie."

Churchill's fear that the sending of food to the Islands would ultimately benefit the occupiers was not unfounded. Although the Germans were very strict in seeing that their troops did not touch the Red Cross parcels, they believed they were entitled to requisition from the Islanders anything that they produced. The Bailiff protested against this unavailingly.

However, food conditions for the German forces were becoming increasingly desperate. The German naval doctor, Dr. Hartmann, wrote:

The discipline of the troops, at least in my district, was first class. I had heard of a young soldier who was shot for having stolen and eaten an islander's dog out of sheer starvation. Once each week the order was read aloud that whoever stole would be shot and this was enforced. It was certainly right that a degree of discipline should exist and that the occupying power should punish and deal harshly with its own subjects in such a way, on the other hand, one saw that the civilian population had more to eat and were supplied with food parcels from the outside by the Red Cross whilst the occupying forces went without.

It was not unknown for soldiers to break into local houses in search of food. On one such occasion, Mrs. Mildred Waddell of 'Samsufi', St. Brelade, was disturbed by a noise in the early morning of 27th December. Going down to investigate, she heard glass breaking and saw the muzzle of a rifle pointing at her. She grabbed the end of it as it went off and was shot in the leg. Sadly, unlike Daphne McCann, she didn't reach hospital until she was taken there by ambulance the following morning, otherwise she might have survived. ACH was called to see her, and at the inquest on 2nd January he made his report, a model of clarity and conciseness. It is noteworthy that, although there was an interval of nine hours between the accident and her admission to hospital, he does not attempt to apportion blame, but lets the facts speak for themselves. He reported:

On the morning of December 27th I was informed that a case of gunshot wound of the leg had been admitted to hospital at 10 am. I examined the lady concerned; she was conscious, and she told me she had been shot by a German soldier at about midnight. She had obviously lost a considerable amount of blood and was considerably shocked. A transfusion of blood was given and an X-ray examination of the leg made. The X-ray showed a compound comminuted fracture of the right thigh, just below the hip joint. There were several pieces of what appeared to be metal visible. About 4 pm her condition was improved sufficiently for an operation. There were three wounds, two of which communicated with the fractured bone, and one of these (the uppermost) appeared to be entirely separate. This would suggest that at least two shots were fired. The wounds were cleaned and the bones were replaced in position as far as possible. No attempt was made to search for the bullet in view of her serious condition. The leg was splinted.

Her condition after the operation was fair, and the following morning somewhat improved, but she collapsed and died suddenly at 9.40 pm on the 28th December, probably from delayed shock. There was no scorching of the wound, but there was considerable bruising. I cannot say from what distance the bullets were fired. She lost so much blood that she did not recover from shock.

Following the incident, Detective Constable Shenton of St. Helier contacted Centenier Le Rossignol of St. Brelade. As the house was in the military zone, Le Rossignol instructed Shenton to telephone the *Geheimefeldpolizei* to meet him at the house. The matter was investigated but no culprit could be found. After the Liberation, British Intelligence took up the affair and interviewed all the German personnel in the area, who were brought to London from their prison camps for interrogation. The suspects were reduced to three. Of these, one had been shot as a deserter later in the war, one, from the Russian brigade, had been returned to Russia, where he would likewise have been shot. The third suspect, from his track record, was the most likely culprit, but there was insufficient evidence to secure a conviction. The matter was dropped.

Chapter 12
1945
The Year of Liberation

According to Sinel the island inhabitants began the year in an upbeat mood. The Red Cross ship *Vega* was now making regular visits, and people were optimistic that the war would soon be over. The Bailiff, however, sounded a note of caution and encouraged everyone to regard their parcels as iron rations and to make them last as long as possible. Rations were running at 1,137.5 calories a day, compared to 3,500 in Britain at the time.

However, this did not prevent the reduction of rations on 15th January, to no butter, and a meat ration every alternate week. The milk ration to the adult population was reduced to half a pint on four days a week, although children and those on special rations had more.

Urgently needed medical supplies took up about half of the shipping space, but the shippers had not always made the best use of the space available. Elise Cathro remembers the supplies stacked at the back of the Hospital near the mortuary, where the medical students had been deputed by ACH to guard them. She was astounded to discover that, amongst the medicaments supplied were slimming pills, seasick tablets, and laxative cereals, just looking like ordinary cereals. These last named looked harmless enough and some of the medical students, finding some of the boxes broken open, felt they were justified in eating some, and suffered the consequences! Elise reflected: "It was criminal, because there were lots of things that were desperately needed."

Baron von Aufsess in his diary reveals the *"Angst"* of a member of the German officer corps in dealing with the Nazis in his midst. He recorded in his diary "How fortunate for all concerned that the enemy decided not to root out the canker in the body politic, the occupying forces, at sword's point, but instead to send a ministering angel to their compatriots in the shape of the Red Cross ship.

Von Aufsess recorded his concern at the large numbers of trees being cut down to provide much needed fuel for the cold and starving inhabitants. In the second week of January he wrote of the felling of the "wonderful evergreen oaks along Victoria Avenue" by local people armed with saws and axes. He continues:

I at once started taking identity cards and confiscating axes and saws. But the numbers were so great and perhaps, too, as my fury increased my sympathy with these poor freezing people increased, and I abandoned the task. The rest of them departed looking crestfallen, leaving the ravaged avenue as a backdrop to the sorry scene… There are plenty of places on the island where timber could have been felled for civilian requirements, without lasting damage. But the decimation of this beautiful avenue is an irreparable loss to the island. It will be fifty years at least before the trees can again reach the stature and fantastic shape which lent the avenue its special charm.

The area to which he refers, between the upper and lower roads, has never been replanted.

But he was clear that their defeat was not far off. He wrote:

The incurable optimists among us still profess to believe in an ultimately favourable outcome to the war. If they really believe this what crises of conscience must they be suffering? Would not an ultimate victory for Hitler now be worse than defeat?

His wife was now imprisoned in Dachau Concentration Camp. He continues:

My wife can now only be freed by the advancing Russians or the advancing Americans. If Hitler were to triumph after all, we should neither of us have anything to look forward to in our own country but humiliation and prison, perhaps the gallows.

At home the German sense of humour was suggesting that when it was all over all one would need to go round Hitler's famous "Thousand Year Reich" was a bicycle.

On 28th February the Islands received a new Commandant. Following the plot on Hitler's life he no longer trusted the Army, and in particular the aristocratic members of the German officer corps who had never been party members. Von Schmettow, who had won the respect of the Islanders for his fair dealing, was replaced by the Naval Commander, Hüffmeier, (now promoted to Admiral). A Nazi zealot, he was not going to take matters lying down and was extremely unpopular with the men. In his speech to the troops in the Forum Cinema he stated:

The first duty of a fortress is not to be captured by the enemy. I mean to hold out here with you till the victory is won.

On 9th March the *Vega* arrived with another consignment of cargo. Amongst the cargo was a package for the General Hospital containing wax impressions for making artificial legs. Mavis Wills, then seventeen, had suffered a terrible accident when only 21 months old. At the time, in August, 1930, her parents lived at the cottage of Pont Marquet House, St. Brelade, near the level crossing where the Jersey Railway climbed up to Don Bridge on the way to Corbière. Mavis was playing in the garden with the other children, it had begun to rain and they were all called inside, the older ones being told to bring little Mavis with them. They omitted to do this and Mavis wandered on to the track holding a flag intending to stop the train and sat down. The train came round the corner and could not stop in time. The engine ran over Mavis's legs and she was terribly injured. Taken to hospital she survived and as she grew up needed artificial legs to fit every stage of her growth.

At first she was fitted with wooden stumps with which she cheerfully went to school on weekdays, Brownies on Saturdays and Sunday School on Sundays. As there were no facilities locally, she had to go over with her mother to the mainland by boat from time to time to be fitted with new legs. When the Occupation started this was obviously no longer possible and she had difficulty getting around. A friend made a kind of side-car for attachment to a bicycle, and the German *Kommandant* gave special permission for her to be carried on her mother's bicycle, in contravention of the current regulations.

Then, in July, 1943 a message from the Red Cross arrived enquiring whether she required replacement legs. ACH cycled to their home in St. Brelade. As he arrived, she was on her knees, playing in the garden, and of course he immediately knew it was her he had come to see. When I went to see Mavis, she remembered him as "stern, but very kind." He explained to her parents why he had come to see her and arrangements were made for the new legs to be ordered through the Red Cross.

There now ensued lengthy correspondence between the Jersey *Feldkommandantur*, Geneva, Lisbon and London, but eventually the consignment was agreed and sent. It was handed over on 14th March 1945, twenty-three months later. Baron von Aufsess comments:

This was surely for a worthy cause and showed we were not indifferent to the needs of the poor and handicapped. But as we unwrapped the parcel to check the contents, a security measure imposed by the conditions of war, the Bailiff could not resist sarcastically quipping that it might contain explosives. There are times when his abrasive manner and lack of good taste are positively obnoxious.

Mavis, who was 15 when the measurements were taken, was now 17, and had obviously grown a good deal in height. The measurements were now wrong. However, with some adjustments, the new legs were fitted nevertheless, and Mavis was now able to get about properly.

Another of my father's patients, Ted Single, had a TB spine and was on his back for $3^1/_2$ years. He said of him: "He was very good, he used to tell me what was wrong with me." But when the time came for him to walk again, he found ACH could be very stern, "like a sergeant-major," and he said to Ted: "Come on you can do it!" Ted was holding on to a nurse, and they collapsed in a heap on the floor, with the nurse on top of Ted. "You're not fit enough for that yet!" ACH said.

Shortly after this von Aufsess was summoned to move to Guernsey. With his wife already in the hands of the *Gestapo*, he recorded in his diary his anxiety that this might mean a signal from Germany for his arrest. He now prepared to put into effect the contingency plan he had prepared, when he received news from an impeccable source that the authorities had nothing against him and his posting was just part of a general reshuffle. He was within only a few hours of leaving from Gorey with his two Jersey friends on 16th April when, to their very great disappointment, he called it off. Hüffmeier explained the reasons for his transfer with reference to the conflict of interests between the occupiers and the Bailiff. Von Aufsess wrote:

As an exponent of compromise it was time I was removed from my post on account of the Bailiff there, who would certainly notice the change. One could not wage war without standing up a few recalcitrants against the wall.

In recording his farewell from Jersey on 19th April he made clear his different opinions of the Bailiff (Coutanche) and the Attorney-General (Duret Aubin). He referred to the expressions of sorrow at his departure which came from them and added that in the case of Duret Aubin he felt they were genuine. He concludes: "As the car left, Ralph Mollet, the Bailiff's secretary, gave a final wave and called 'We shall remember you, you were a gentleman.'"

Prayers Answered

An interesting parallel to the Roman Catholic mass held in Jersey the previous year on the feast of Christ the King is provided at a church parade held in Guernsey that Easter. It was 1st April, and the new supremo, Admiral Hüffmeier, was present. The Chaplain was Pastor Wilhelm Burkert, ordained in the Evangelical Church of the Rhineland and a Lieutenant in the Army. He tells in *Channel Islands Occupation Review No.26*, of an encounter he had with him that day, which highlights the moral dilemma which believers serving in the *Wehrmacht* faced with regard to the oath of allegiance each of them had to swear to Adolf Hitler. This was a very significant factor for those Christians plotting against Hitler in the lead up to the attempt on his life the previous year.

During the sermon, he maintained a steady gaze directed at me. And, on Easter Monday he enquired whether I would have time to visit him. His first question was: 'What can the pastors working amongst the troops do to strengthen their resolve to survive and resist the enemy?' I answered: 'Nothing.' - to which Admiral Hüffmeier retorted: 'But we can strengthen the conscience that binds us to our oath of allegiance.' (I was as this time unaware of how many officers were questioning the oath of allegiance that they had made, binding them to their loyalty to Hitler). Our discussion lasted for several hours, during which the Admiral made reference to the pastors in his family. Several days later, the Admiral called a meeting of representatives of all units, in the large auditorium of the Regal Cinema, at which he himself spoke, declaring: 'Christians, do not scorn my words: you are bound by conscience to keep your oath.' This summed up the influence of the National-Socialist political officers who, like the commissars of the Russian army, were responsible for the ideological loyalty of the troops.

Burkert records how the effects of hunger at that time had a spiritual effect:

There were groups among our number who gathered for Bible study. As a result of their times of fasting, they experienced ever increasing evidence of God's power, which was revealed to them directly. The expression and intensity of the pastors' belief was transformed. Equally, ever increasing numbers of those attending services found faith, and their lives were changed. This was evident in many letters sent to their homes. As the German Reich collapsed, God built his kingdom.

In Jersey, similar things were happening. Ernst Kämpfer, a staff sergeant with the Army Engineers, and a keen Christian of the Lutheran Church, used to lead Bible classes in St. Helier Church, whenever it was possible, for any soldiers of similar beliefs. This usually involved the troops in extra kit inspections, or similar chores, but Ernst was not to be discouraged: "I did not care," he said, "I was not going to be turned away from my beliefs." As conditions grew worse, and food supplies dwindled, the spectre of starvation drew nearer. Ernst and his prayer group prayed to God to send them some food. On 18th February there was a huge storm and hundreds of dead squid were washed up on St. Ouen's Bay. Ernst concluded: "We ate squid cooked in every way you could think of for some ten days afterwards. But God had answered our prayers!"

In Guernsey, on the eve of the capitulation on 8th May, the Battery Commander in the St. Sampson's area, a devout Catholic, invited Pastor Burkert and another officer to conduct a service for their unit, in St. Sampson's Church. He preached on Hosea chapter 6, verse 1:

Come let us return to the Lord. He has torn us to pieces, but he will heal us; he had injured us, but he will bind up our wounds.

After the service Pastor Burkert wrote in the service register:

I give thanks for all the dear Christians who we have come to know during our time in Guernsey, in this house of God. May the Lord lead the world to the eternal destination of his heavenly kingdom, and may he create a peace that is greater than any human purpose - through Jesus Christ, ever the same, yesterday, today and in eternity. Signed: Oberleutnant Burkert, pastor of Waldenburg in Silesia.

In all the Islands the months leading up to the Liberation saw rising expectations on the part of the civilian population, and amongst the occupiers quiet resignation on the part of the non-party members and increasing fanaticism on the part of the party members. By the end of the month the situation reached such a pitch that von Aufsess and Lt. Colonel Helldorf began seriously to question their duty of loyalty to their Commander-in-Chief. Hüffmeier was getting more and more extreme in his views, declaring that he would never accept unconditional surrender, and that if surrender were unavoidable he would blow up all the arms and ammunition in the Islands. Von Aufsess asked himself what had happened to his moral scruples that he even contemplated killing the man in cold blood. He confessed that this decision had only been reached after long sleepless nights, but he had reached a position where he was resolved to compromise no longer with "these enemies of humanity."

And so Helldorf offered to assassinate Hüffmeier, and planned to do so on one of the Admiral's regular visits to his mess in Castle Cornet. However, events moved on and the plan was never put into operation

On 20th April Hitler's birthday was celebrated by a speech given by the Admiral. Von Aufsess records:

He is certainly a worthy pupil of Goebbels [the Nazi propaganda minister]. The Realkino, where the big gathering of troops was held, was decked out in the best Nazi tradition, huge flags, floodlights, attendant orchestra, etc. The Admiral and his adjutant, so sadly lacking in inches, appeared on the platform as 'the long and the short of it.' Hüffmeier snapped smartly to attention and greeted the assembly with a loud 'Heil Hitler', which was vociferously returned.

Taking his stand on the rostrum, he allowed half a minute to elapse in solemn silence. Then this scion of a family of Protestant pastors began his National Socialist sermon, speaking with evangelical fervour, but on behalf of Adolf instead of God. He spoke, too, with consummate skill, first engaging the common sentiments of his listeners, then speaking frankly, glossing nothing over, the more compellingly to carry them away on a final surge of emotion... I was not myself entirely immune to its appeal. But the critical faculty intervened and after half an hour I could only feel mounting fury at this meretricious and deceptive show.

In Jersey, von Aufsess had been replaced as *Feldkommandant* by Captain von Cleve, who took the rank of *Platzkommandant*. Coutanche speaks well of him as "a remarkable person", a "very easy man to deal with, and we got on very well."

According to Coutanche, at this stage the Germans stated they wished him to have a wireless set, and in fact provided him with one.

Von Aufsess presents a rather different picture:

What is plaguing (von Cleve) at the moment is the growing insolence and importunity of the Bailiff of Jersey. Coutanche is now demanding that, as a gesture of goodwill, we should abdicate at least a part of our control over island affairs, as he cannot otherwise guarantee the maintenance of peace and good order. He also suggests that it would be expedient to lift the ban on listening to the BBC. This is all subterfuge on his part and designed to increase his own prestige and standing with the population. With the end of the Occupation in sight he is clearly determined to emerge as the strong and popular leader.

People were beginning to taunt the soldiers. Von Aufsess advised von Cleve to issue a warning notice to the people, urging calm, and dictated a text to him. Coutanche insisted on seeing the Admiral, who arrived from Guernsey on 5th May. The upshot of the visit was that, as Coutanche put it: "The Admiral agreed that I should make a reassuring statement to the Islanders."

That morning a German soldier shot and killed himself in a lavatory in the General Hospital.

Chapter 13
"So it is Finished"

The end, when it came, was a rather drawn out affair. As in the case of the *Wehrmacht* five years before, elaborate plans were drawn up for a large scale military assault by the British in the event of the surrender not going ahead as planned. Operation 'Nestegg' was alerted on 3rd May and a radio message was sent to the German Command in the Channel Islands stating that General Officer Commanding, Southern Command was authorised to receive unconditional surrender. It was not until 6th May that a reply was received stating that "the Commander-in-Chief, Channel Islands, receives orders only from his own government."

The following day the unconditional surrender of the German High Command was received and all active operations were to cease at one minute past midnight on 9th May. On the afternoon of 8th May Churchill broadcast to the nation, giving details of the surrender arrangements and adding that in the interests of saving lives the ceasefire was already being sounded on the whole front the same day. It was heard over loudspeakers which had been hurriedly erected in various parts of St. Helier, and throughout the Hospital loudspeaker system. Betty Thurban was in St. Helier, by the Opera House to listen to the speech. She re-entered the Hospital, and found herself in the lift with a German soldier. "Thank God it's all over," he said to her. She warmly agreed.

Although postal services were not restored until 15th May, my father wrote to my mother even as the liberators were landing, and managed to find means to have his letters posted on the mainland. His correspondence bears all the marks of the thrill and chaos of those days:

May 9th *Dearest*

So it is finished. I have often wondered during the last five years how it would and of course I [have] been wrong as usual. The tension during the last few days has been unbearable and I am still in a kind of dream. Up to the last minute the mad Nazi Admiral has refused to give in and waited to make this place the last fortress under the German flag. Even yesterday he told the Bailiff:

'Yes, I know the British government will announce that the war is at an end, but that is nothing to do with me. They would have to take it by storm.'

But now our ships are in the bay and our fighters are cruising overhead. Captain Richardson [a peacetime mailboat captain] (you remember him), piloted the destroyers here. What a thrill for Michael that it should finish on his birthday. [Indeed, I hung a Jersey flag out of the dayroom in our school!]

We have been in a pretty poor way lately, but I'll tell you all about it when I can think coherently. Hope you got some of the letters I smuggled out… I've heard no news of a mail yet, but am posting this in case the Destroyer leaves tonight.

I'm fine and longing to see you all. Sorry this is rather an incoherent first letter. My love, dearest, Arthur.

He wrote again the following day:

Thursday *Dearest*

What a day! I still feel very dazed, but I'll try to write a coherent letter. During the last 48 hours I've had practically no sleep and have lived chiefly on alcohol. At the moment I'm sitting in the dining room, having just finished a meal of bread and cheese. Donald and I have been foraging for souvenirs and the Newberys [Mrs. Lock and Audrey] are out painting the Town red. Donald, by the way, is an escaped prisoner we've had for a couple of months. We've just collected some helmets, rifles, etc.

But I'm starting at the wrong end, like Alice in Wonderland.

As I told you in my first, hurried note, there was tension up to the end. Nobody knew if the mad Admiral would surrender, and apparently there were conflicting orders. We have just heard the B.B.C. account of the negotiations.

For 24 hours after we had heard that they had decided to give in, nothing happened. Then they released the political prisoners and handed over the civil government to the Bailiff. Still our people gave no sign. Then at 3-0 the Bailiff spoke and we put up all the flags. It was marvellous to see them spring out immediately after Winnie's speech [a popular wartime name for Winston Churchill]. I heard it at the Hospital. Still our people did not come and the first night passed with the Germans walking about fully armed, smiling complacently. Crowds of people rushed about waving flags and letting off fireworks. We woke up next morning expecting to hear planes or see something. But it was still Occupied Jersey.

Then in the late morning a Destroyer steamed across the Bay and dropped anchor. Apparently the German Commander went aboard and signed the surrender. The Town filled and the Germans sat about and watched the crowds. Cars appeared from their hiding places as if by magic (I had the Rover), and everybody crowded down to the harbour. Presently a launch came ashore and the Colonel, with a small escort landed and hauled down the Nazi flag from their headquarters at the Pomme d'Or [Hotel], while another party led by Le Brocq of the Militia, went up to the Fort [Regent] and hoisted the Union Jack. Landing craft appeared and the troops came ashore. This was a Task Force expecting trouble and quite prepared for it. But the Germans were too cowed to make trouble. The first men ashore were mobbed and they just cannot get over their reception. They say they never anticipated anything approaching it. (Why I don't know). The whole of the population crowded round the Pomme d'Or and Royal Square. Then the planes came over and that was the most impressive sight of all - Thunderbolts first, followed by Mosquitoes. Four years ago I saw the air black with German planes and this impressed me more than anything.

While all this was going on I decided to organise a dance at the Hospital. We fixed it up within the hour and all the nurses brought out their evening frocks. We got the Swiss Red Cross representatives who arrived a few days ago and they made a great sensation. But about the middle of the evening a Major and several of the officers came along and the nurses nearly went mad with excitement. We raided the store and served out champagne and had the toast from Cavalcade. I shall never forget it and I got back at 4.15.

This morning I went round with the RAMC [Royal Army Medical Corps] Captain and we are turning the Germans out of the part of the hospital they have had for four years. I went round to the mess this afternoon and collected a much needed razor blade and had a jolly good meal of sardines and Army biscuits. And so to bed.

Sunday

There is still no arrangement about mails but I think I can send this off via Pirouet - now a Commander RNR and second in command of the convoy. All yesterday and today they have been unloading food and medical supplies from those amazing landing craft which ran up the beach by First Tower.

I have had a hectic two days and if I look a wreck when I see you it will be 'liberation' and not occupation.

About 8 MOs [medical officers] have arrived, including young Ferguson. They have cleared the Jerries out of the Hospital and we hope to move into our old wards as soon as it has been cleaned up. It was filthy as were all the places occupied by the Jerries.

There is still no word about arrangements for our getting away and it may be some time. In fact some people think it will be easier for you to come to me. On the other hand one of the RAMC fellows - the surgeon - thinks I may get early permission to go in order to learn about penicillin etc.

We are still rather dazed by our new freedom and I shall have to curb my instinct to disobey laws and regulations. The shadow of the Gestapo [sic.] still hangs over us, but I suppose it will lift in time. They have rounded up all the Gestapo and most of them will hang. We have got into such odd habits of secrecy - speaking in whispers, looking round before we speak, hiding things etc.

I'm afraid this letter is rather incoherent: there is so much to say that I don't know where to begin. But I must leave this with Blomp [Dr. Blampied] as he will deliver it to Pirouet. Good bye my dear, I can't settle down to anything until I know you are all safe.

When Churchill announced that "our dear Channel Islands" were to be "freed today" he had not taken account of the delaying tactics of the fanatical Admiral Hüffmeier. A signal was sent to Hüffmeier in Guernsey proposing a rendezvous four miles south of Les Hanois light to sign an instrument of surrender. This was agreed for midday on 8th May.

With the help of the BBC recordings of the time we shall see how the situation unravelled. HMS *Bulldog*, with HMS *Beagle*, left Plymouth at 10.00 am. In the *Bulldog* was Brigadier Snow, with two officers and 20 other ranks, and a similar complement sailed on the *Beagle*, to land in Guernsey and Jersey, respectively. A rendezvous was made with a German mine-sweeping trawler. An officer was rowed over, and climbed up the gangway, his dignity somewhat impaired by the fact that he was dripping wet from the waist down. He was received with due honours and piped on board. In return he gave the Heil Hitler salute; his papers were examined by the interpreter and he was taken to the wardroom. The BBC correspondent on the *Bulldog* recalled how the officer, *Kapitänleutnant* Armin Zimmermann, of the 46th Minesweeping Flotilla was "tense and nervous" as he faced Brigadier Snow, explained that he was not empowered to sign any surrender and emphasised that he was only authorised to discuss armistice terms. He added that the armistice did not come into force until one minute after midnight. Brigadier Snow made it clear to him that there was no question of an armistice. They had come, he said, for unconditional surrender. Zimmerman was told to withdraw and was then called back a few minutes later to be told that he would be returned to the shore with a copy of the surrender document in English and German. He was told that another rendezvous should be arranged immediately. The correspondent noted how

Zimmermann swallowed nervously, shifted uneasily and added in a low voice 'I am commanded to add that if you do not move your ships immediately, your presence here will be construed as an unfriendly action.' Silence followed, Zimmermann was told to withdraw, gave the Nazi salute, and was ushered to a cabin, and kept waiting for an hour while the instructions for the new rendezvous were prepared.

Zimmermann returned to the shore and *Bulldog* withdrew out of range of the coastal batteries and patrolled the Guernsey coast for six hours.

This piece of Nazi playacting infuriated von Aufsess who wrote in his diary:

The Admiral in a silly fit of pique and pride, at first threatened to fire on the English ships when they arrived a few hours before the agreed time. The ships withdrew, but he thus lost his one and only chance of negotiation and merely angered the victorious enemy. To exacerbate them further, his envoy the theatrical Lieut Commander Zimmermann, sent to make the first contact aboard the leading British ship, greeted its commander with upflung arm and the Hitler salute. One can only guess at the feelings of the astounded British officer, but must assume that for once the English response to the comical failed, and he was both offended and outraged... With one foolish gesture of defiance, all the goodwill earned by the troops in years of exemplary behaviour had been destroyed.

Admiral Hüffmeier, probably unwilling to face the music, but under the pretext of military unrest in the Island, deputed the Guernsey Commandant, Major-General Heine, to sign for him. Aufsess remembers him as "A decent and honourable old man, meticulously correct in his conduct." As Colonel Heine he had previously held the post of Fortress Commander in Jersey. Aufsess commenting on his appointment to take over command of the troops in Guernsey, writes:

Rather a come down and probably painful for him, but he is shortly to be compensated by promotion to General. His decency and justice are beyond doubt and have won him universal regard.

A rendezvous was fixed for midnight plus one minute just outside St. Peter Port to receive Heine, who would sign unconditional surrender on behalf of the German Commander-in-Chief. Heine was accompanied by "our old friend Captain Zimmermann," as the BBC correspondent humourously referred to him, and who was doubtless deputed by the Admiral to keep an eye on Heine. The General was piped aboard the *Bulldog*, gave the conventional salute, and showed his documents. "Tired and drawn" he was shown to the wardroom. The interpreter spoke first: "Can you please tell us who you are." He replied, with deference and dignity, "I am Major-General Heine. I am the representative of the Commandant Fortress Jersey and the Supreme Commander in Guernsey." After questioning him closely on various points, Brigadier Snow addressed him in English: "I understand you have come here to make unconditional surrender." The interpreter translated; he replied: *"Ich bin dazu ermässigt"*, "I am so authorised." Snow continued: "Of all the German forces, and all the collective personnel, in the Channel Islands." Heine replied in a low voice, briefly, *"Ja."* "And of all their equipment?" *"Ja."* "And that you will accept my orders?" *"Ja."* Heine then returned to the shore.

The *Bulldog* then sailed, piloted by a German marine, till she stood just off the harbour entrance. Here the act of surrender was signed at 7.14 am on 9th May. On the quarter deck the naval guard was formed up in a square, and Brigadier Snow and Major-General Heine faced each other across a flat topped table placed on a naval barrel. Snow read out: "The German Commander in the Channel Islands agrees to surrender unconditionally." Heine, with conviction, *"Jawohl"*. And you, Major-General Heine, are his representative? Heine, wearily, *"Jawohl"*.

Snow, clearly in charge but with the smooth urbanity of a senior bank official overseeing the signature of an important transaction, continued:

I wish you now to sign the instrument of surrender. I must ask you to sign a copy for the British Government, a copy for the United States Government, a copy for the Soviet Government, a copy for me, a copy for my General and a copy for you. There are two German copies.

Final instructions were given for all German flags to be taken down. Brigadier Snow then sailed to Jersey in the *Beagle* to take the separate surrender of the Island Commandant and Divisional Commander, Major-General Wulf, arriving there at 10.00 am. A German vessel, the FK01, went out to meet it, but Wulf was not on board, and an order was given for his immediate attendance.

Meanwhile, Bailiff Coutanche had received a message from the Harbour Office to the effect that the *Beagle* was rounding Noirmont Point, and that he was to meet Major-General Wulf at the German Naval Headquarters, the Pomme d'Or Hotel, at noon. On appearing, he saw that Wulf was accompanied by two staff officers. Clearly not wanting to be upstaged, he made the General wait while he summoned the Attorney-General and Solicitor General. On their arrival on board the *Beagle* Brigadier Snow expressed to Wulf his severe displeasure at being kept waiting and, brushing his "arrogant" protests aside, nearly reduced the man to tears.

The surrender was duly signed, Coutanche sent loyal greetings to His Majesty King George VI, and then he and Wulf returned to shore at 2.00 pm.

A pinnace, carrying two British naval officers, Surgeon Lieutenant McDonald and Sub Lt. Milne, sailed into St. Helier Harbour, passing the Bailiff and Wulf on their way out. On arrival, the officers (who had been sent ahead to assess whether there was any contagious disease among the population) were carried shoulder high to the Harbour Office where they hung out the Union flag. The advance party of troops then followed, and at 3.40 pm the British flag was raised on the Pomme d'Or Hotel. At. 4.20 pm, Major Hugh Le Brocq of the Royal Jersey Militia entered Fort Regent and raised the flag over St. Helier, and the main landing party arrived at 5.00 pm.

The populace flocked to St. Helier to welcome the first landing parties. Audrey Goodwin remembers:

Then at the end, I saw the English warships come into the bay and then all the soldiers came. Everybody went down to the harbour. I was there and I saw them on the balcony of the Pomme d'Or and then they were in the square, and everybody was cheering.

At the Physiotherapy Department one of the regular patients turned up as usual for her treatment. Elise Floyd (Cathro) was trying to pluck up courage to tell her that today the Hospital was celebrating, not treating, when ACH came along and said: "Don't you realise the war has ended, we aren't doing any work today," and strode off. And so they celebrated that night.

In Berlin, my uncle Captain Christopher Goode, celebrated the end of the war by "liberating" a Nazi flag from the German *Reichstag*. He had it cut up into a dress for his wife Wendy and decorated it all over with white hearts. He also took an Iron Cross which he gave to me. About that time his lorry was in collision with one belonging to the Red Army. The Russian officer was most polite and apologetic and exclaimed: "You shoot your driver and I'll shoot mine!" Needless to say Christopher declined the offer.

In Somerset, my mother stayed at home instead of celebrating with her friends in the vain hope that my father might telephone. Unfortunately, civilian telephonic communication was not restored for another two months.

Ray Osmont continues with the story:

After all the staff had gathered in the main hall to hear Churchill's speech, Arthur Halliwell asked me to organise a dance for the nurses and medical staff, auxiliaries and GPs. This included four young and recent Old Victorians [from the local public school, Victoria College] who were attending hospital rounds as prospective medical students: Peter Falla, to become a local GP, John Watson who rose to senior consultative position as an orthopaedic specialist in the UK, [where he pioneered work on hip replacement], Noël Blackwell who worked as a radiographer in the X-Ray Department before going to the UK into general practice, and Frank Keiller (formerly Killer) who set up in Australia. ACH leaned on the GPs and his friends and provided the wine.

At St. James's Church, the Vicar arranged a service of thanksgiving which, despite the short notice, was very well attended. Then that evening he, with his two daughters were invited with my father and Dr. McKinstry to dine with Harold Blampied. Elise remembers: "We had a great meal and opened the champagne which had been saved for the occasion." It was Harold who had first encouraged ACH to settle in the Island, and, like my father he had sent his family to England for the duration.

Then the next evening the staff gathered in the Hospital for their celebration dance. They danced to a three piece band led by Ernie L'Amy from 9.30 pm till 8.00 am the next day.

Dr. Osmont concludes:

During the evening, at ACH's prompting I tried to persuade the German resident surgeon to join us for a short while but he was adamant that he would not. Some time after midnight, both of us, armed with a bottle of brandy found the German in his quarters. He eventually agreed to join us in a drink and we drank to an acceptable toast of the common ground of the medical profession. I recount this story merely to exemplify the stature of Arthur Halliwell whose patriotism throughout these five years was fervent to say the least. I can only add that to me, as a young medical student, his sense of duty to his patients and the example he set to all his colleagues was a guide for so many of us in our future careers.

That evening ACH exclaimed: "Come to my house on Friday, we'll have a party there." Elise Floyd (Cathro) was due to pick up the officers who had joined them, at the Pomme d'Or Hotel and take them up to 'Le Clos du Chemin'. She tells what happened next:

I went with Dr. McKinstry in his car to pick up these two officers. When we got there, there was no light in the hotel, so they said they were busy for a little while and showed us into an empty office next door and told us to wait. Suddenly the door opened and a man came in in pyjamas and dressing gown and came up to the desk. He suddenly looked up and saw me sitting there. 'Good God,' he said at the top of his voice, 'there's a woman in my office.' The officers came rushing in through the communicating door. In the meantime he turned to me, bowed and said: 'Madam, I am Colonel Robinson, commanding His Majesty's forces in the island.' Apparently the Colonel had gone to bed, and the junior officers, thinking he was safely in bed, had put us in his office. In fact Colonel Robinson had come down to check on the arrangements for the landing of the bulk of the troops at West Park. So he said to us: 'Well, you might as well stay now.' So we heard all the revision of the plans for the landing of the troops. And then we went out to 'Le Clos du Chemin' for the party. We had a great party; we rolled up the carpet in the drawing room and danced to a wind up gramophone. And there was food, he must have got it from somewhere!

One of the landing craft which beached the next day in St. Aubin's Bay was specially equipped with medical facilities. On 12th May a field ambulance of the British Liberation Army was set up in the back yard of the Hospital buildings under the command of Major Portman, Royal Army Medical Corps. Within a short space of time he had re-instated the Hospital as a civilian Hospital. The German resident Medical Officer was ordered to remove stretcher cases, wheelchair patients, walking wounded and orderlies out to the grounds of the Hospital, and they proceeded to the waiting transport for shipment to England. The following morning the Hospital was handed over to the Matron, and the Field Ambulance moved out of the hospital buildings to another location.

Amongst those disembarking was a gentleman in civilian clothes, wearing a bowler hat and carrying a rolled umbrella. Some thought he was something to do with civilian administration. But later he was to make himself known.

Medical student Frank Killer had helped organise a resistance group. One of the hospital porters called him to say that there was a gentleman who wished to speak to him. Frank explains:

He was waiting in the front hall. We shook hands. I can't remember if he introduced himself, but if he did I didn't note his name. He was tall and wore a bowler hat and an expensive looking coat. He had a furled umbrella. He carried himself like a soldier and looked distinguished. He was well fed and not like the rest of us. He didn't look like we did after five years of occupation. He said:

'On behalf of British Intelligence, thank you for what you and your friends did.'

He shook hands again, turned on his heels and disappeared. I have never seen or heard of him since. I don't think I said a single word.

Meetings were held with the Army medical authorities to ascertain the immediate needs of the Hospital. During one such meeting, a 'phone message arrived to tell my father that a letter, the first since 1940, had arrived from my mother, and that his housekeeper had cycled in with it. They had asked him how many trusses were needed. My father plucked a figure out of the air and departed to read the letter. The following day the Army rang up to query the figure they had been given. Irritated by the question, ACH said that of course it was correct. In due course twelve crates of trusses arrived, far beyond anything that was likely to be needed. To his credit my father was happy to tell this story against himself!

The Operating Theatre having been handed back, Betty Thurban was deputed to prepare it for use. To her surprise she found herself on her knees, removing all the caked blood with which the floor was covered.

How many years were to pass before the effects of these five tragic years of bloodshed were to be healed, both in Britain and in Germany?

Reflecting on those five years Betty said:

People say it was terrible, and in a way it was. It was strange because you learnt an awful lot of things. It did one no harm to have to put up with such things.

However, a healing process was already under way. Von Aufsess concludes his diary with the following comment:

When the first reporters arrived and asked the Bailiff of Guernsey and President Leale to tell them something about the behaviour of the German troops during the Occupation, both replied that it had been exemplary. The reporters protested that the time was hardly right for the publication of such news and it was not what their readers had expected. Both these honourable men remained adamant in defending their view and the reporters were forced to retire, disappointed and in disarray.

My diary must close with this final tribute to British fair play.

Or, as my father summed it up to a relative. When asked how he got on with the Germans he replied: "If you treated them well, they treated you well." He also admitted to one benefit the Occupation had brought: "The Germans taught the Jerseyman to brew decent beer, and occasionally I managed to get some on the side!

Clearing up

The Liberation was an end, it was also a beginning: the beginning of a new era in international relations. For a while it seemed that with the arrival of peace, all the nation's troubles were over. But when Winston Churchill affirmed his desire to meet our Russian Allies as far east as possible, he was pointing the nation in the direction of the conflict which was to fill most of the remaining years of the twentieth century, the "Cold War" with Communism. At Yalta on the Black Sea, the leaders of the Allied nations met to draw up their plan for the future shape of Europe. Germany was divided into four zones of occupation, one each for Britain, France, America and the Soviet Union. From that moment on each of those zones was under the political tutelage of the occupying power. Whilst democratic developments were encouraged in the three Western zones, the Soviet Zone was firmly linked to a Communist bloc which extended from the border with the West, through the Balkans as far as the border with Russia proper. In each of these countries puppet regimes were installed which danced to Moscow's tune, and a row of barbed wire defences, backed with watch towers, mines and machine-guns was erected from Murmansk in the far north, to the Black Sea in the south. Churchill aptly named it the "Iron Curtain".

At Yalta, agreement was also reached concerning the many prisoners and displaced persons who found themselves outside their homeland at the end of hostilities. The three Western Allies agreed to repatriate any Soviet nationals in their territories and the Russians, for their part, agreed to repatriate British, French and US citizens, many of whom were former prisoners-of-war in German camps, in their territories. The escaped Russian slave workers came into this category, and my father's former protégé, George Kozloff, found himself in the care of the British military in a transit camp near Guildford. Bob Le Sueur told me the rest of George's story:

When liberation came, within ten days a military attaché came from the Soviet embassy to round up the remaining Soviet citizens in the Island. They were in various categories. There were prisoners-of-war, escaped slave workers, like George. There were civilians who were escaped slave workers. There were those still in the work camps, some were military, other civilians. There was a fifth category, Soviet citizens, who had been prisoners-of-war who had volunteered to join the army of General Vlassof, a top Soviet general who had gone over to the German side after being captured, because he was fiercely anti-Marxist. They were called the 'Russian Army of Liberation.' They were based mostly at Les Platons on the north coast which they were responsible for defending. They were mostly given non-combatant jobs. They wore German uniform with a shoulder flash with the letters in Cyrillic, 'POA' for Russian Army of Liberation. (The locals called them 'Pals of Adolf'). To the horror and terror of people like George no note of specific categories was taken when lists of names were being compiled. Those who had fought for the Soviet cause were treated the same as those who had defected to the enemy. The fact that no distinction was made did not augur well for those returning. Part of the Yalta agreement between the West and the Soviet Union specified that all nationals of both sides would be returned, and until the last Western prisoner-of-war was safely home there would be no question of any Russian being able to claim political asylum. The Russian men were horrified to be told by the Russian major that when they were on the way from the port to Guildford to the transit camp where they were to stay they might notice that people would wave to them and might even throw them cigarettes, but they were not to be taken in by this, because these people had been put there to do this to make them think that the English were friendly to them. They knew this was not true, they knew the friendliness was genuine. They were in a transit camp in Guildford and George tried to escape. Apparently he and another man tried to escape and were picked up almost immediately and were put into handcuffs and kept under armed guard until the train was prepared to take them all to Dover. There they were put on a troop ship to Ostend and then another train destined for the Soviet Zone of Germany. George knew perfectly well the moment they reached the Soviet Zone, he, as an officer in the Soviet Army who had attempted to desert would have been shot. At some stage in the night, in August 1945, as the train was crossing Germany he somehow distracted the guard's attention, stood up, kicked him in the fork, put his boot through the window and threw himself out into the night. He was very fit, and knew that he had to let his body go limp. So he rolled down the embankment. To his surprise the train did not stop. He was bruised, made his way through a forest and lay up until day came.

He wanted to make sure he was walking west, not east. George had been kitted out in British army battledress, without any shoulder flashes, and hence no means of identification. He reached a large farm and found it deserted. Many people had fled in anticipation of the Russian arrival. He found a metal post and rubbed his wrists against it until he was free of the handcuffs. He began to walk west, and was picked up by two British soldiers in a Jeep. He told them he was a Pole who had got separated from his unit. They gave him a lift to where they were stationed where he told his story. He was taken to the officer in charge who happened to speak Polish. He tried to persuade him to let him go back to England where, he said, he would be all right and he would get political asylum. The officer explained the terms of the Yalta agreement and that no political asylum could possibly be given until every British soldier in Russian hands had been repatriated. The officer agreed that he could work in the kitchens until he was able to declare himself as a political refugee.

George was impatient to get back to England and he just attached himself to a group of British soldiers going home on leave. When he reached Ostend, having no papers, he was picked up by the Military Police who locked him up for the night. The following morning they put him on a Jeep, without handcuffs, and drove him along the motorway from Ostend to Brussels, intending to take him to the Soviet Embassy. Whether they connived with him is not clear, but when they reached Brussels and the Jeep was held up in traffic lights, he jumped off and ran off until he saw a church, intending to hide in there. Inside the church he saw a small cupboard with curtains and went to hide there.

He found himself in a confessional box. A voice said: 'Oui, mon fils?' George came from that part of Russian society where, before the Revolution many families had French governesses. He spoke French and explained his predicament to the priest. The priest took him up into the belfry and told him to stay there. After dark he returned riding a bicycle and leading another. They left, George following at a discrete distance, to the presbytery. From there he was moved to another presbytery in the country. There he sat it out until he could seek political asylum.

This, he did and ultimately he trained as a teacher of physical education. He met a German woman, and moved with her to Bavaria. He was badly injured, while swimming, by a water skier. He went to a rehabilitation centre where he remained until retirement. He then retired on a teacher's pension and state pension, as well as his German employment and state pension.

Some years later he wrote to two of his Jersey friends asking them to certify that he had been employed by the Organisation Todt from August 1942 till May 1945. This they agreed to do. So George got another three years' credit on his German old age pension. He always refused to be naturalised, always affirming his pride in being Russian.

In later years George revisited Jersey many times.

Surrender conference on board HMS *Bulldog*, 9th May 1945. In the foreground is Admiral Hüffmeier's envoy, the "theatrical" Lieut Commander Zimmermann, and in the centre is Major-General Heine, Fortress Commander of Guernsey. *By courtesy of the Société Jersiaise Photographic Archive, Jersey*

Shortly after midday on 9th May 1945, a naval pinnace carrying the Bailiff (with the raised hat), and the Island Commandant and Divisional Commander, Major-General Wulf, leaves St. Helier Harbour bound for HMS *Beagle* where the surrender documents will be signed. *By courtesy of the Société Jersiaise Photographic Archive, Jersey*

Ecstatic crowds gather outside the Pomme d'Or Hotel to witness British troops raise the Union Jack on the former German Naval Headquarters.
By courtesy of the Société Jersiaise Photographic Archive, Jersey

German prisoners-of-war snake across the sand at West Park, as they leave Jersey by transporter on 19th May 1945. *By courtesy of the Société Jersiaise Photographic Archive, Jersey*

Time to go: the fanatical Admiral Hüffmeier leaves his Guernsey headquarters accompanied by his diminutive Flag Lieutenant, Ewald Severing. Hüffmeier later renounced National Socialism, and became a Lutheran Pastor. *CIOS Collection*

ACH in 1945-"I am tired..."

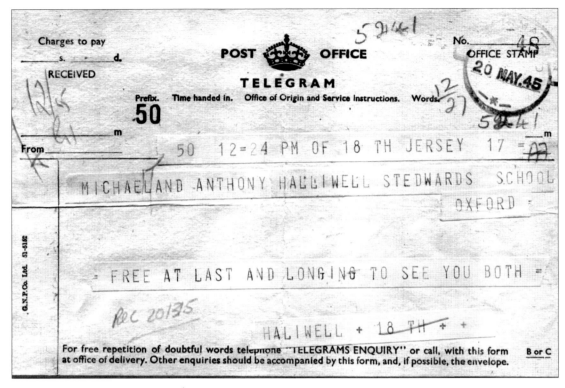

Post Office Telegram dated 18th May 1945, addressed to myself and Anthony: "Free at last and longing to see you both."

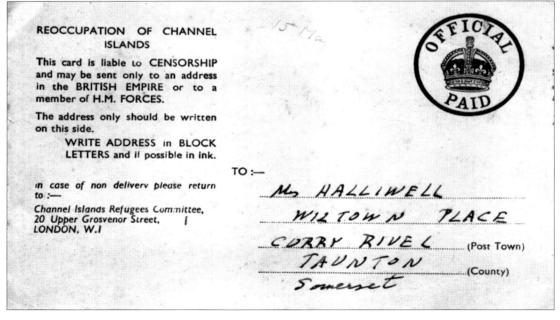

'Re-Occupation of Channel Islands' postcard, front portion.

Full POSTAL ADDRESS of SENDER (in BLOCK LETTERS)

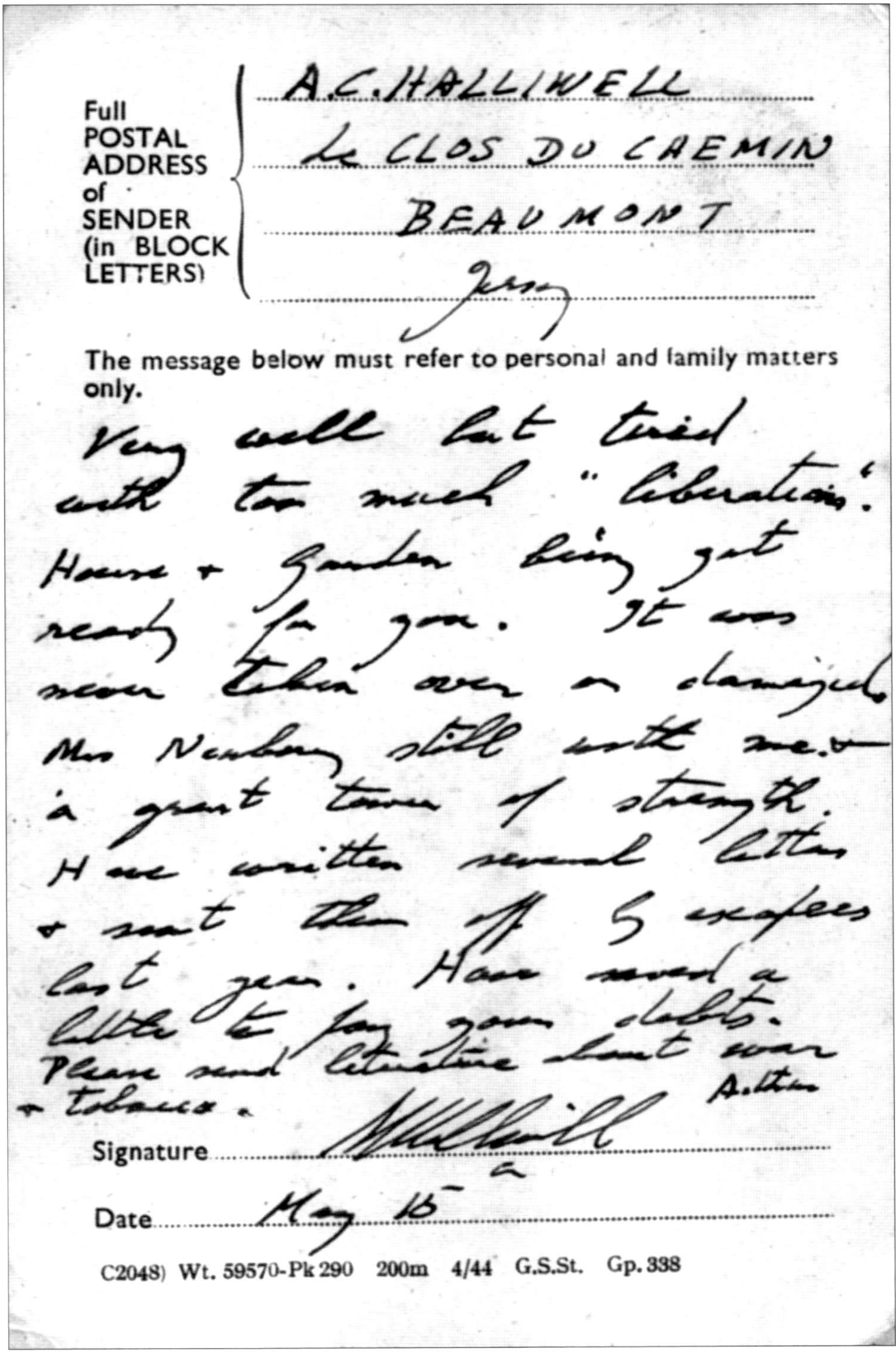

A.C. HALLIWELL
Le CLOS DU CHEMIN
BEAUMONT
Jersey

The message below must refer to personal and family matters only.

Very well but tired with too much "liberation". House & Garden being got ready for you. It was never taken over or damaged. Mrs Newbery still with me & a great tower of strength. Have written several letters & sent them off by escapees last year. Have saved a little to pay your debts. Please send literature about war & tobacco. A. Hallwell

Signature ... Halliwell

Date ... May 15

C2048) Wt. 59570-Pk 290 200m 4/44 G.S.St. Gp. 338

'Re-Occupation of Channel Islands' postcard, reverse.

My sister Daphne and I at the Underground Hospital shortly after the Liberation.

ACH during the late 1950s, with one of his "quizzical" looks.

Nursing and medical staff reunion, May, 1985. Frank Keiller and Peter Falla flank the back row, and Canon Kenneth Preston is on the left of the middle row. Second left in the front row is Averell Darling, and second right is Ray Osmont. *By courtesy of the Société Jersiaise Photographic Archive, Jersey*

Preparing for the Return

Now that the war over, my mother was hopeful that we would all soon be able to return to Jersey; but we were only five of many thousands of Channel Islanders waiting to return to their homes. Some were being demobilised from the Forces, others, like us, were refugees who had left in 1940. Immigration was strictly controlled and passport type documents, called 'Travel Permits', were issued in which visas were stamped, giving permission to travel. These were checked by immigration officials in the Islands and on the mainland.

Shortly after the Liberation, Bailiff Coutanche broadcast to those Islanders in the UK a message which vividly reveals the conditions under which they had been living:

I should like to send a special word of greeting to all Channel Islanders who are in the armed forces of the crown. I want also, although I have already done so in person to the ministers of the crown, to do so tomorrow to His Majesty in person. I should like to express the profound thanks of the Channel Islands, not only for the manner of our liberation, but also for the measure in which help is being brought to us. It is all so wonderful that we can hardly imagine the magnitude of the benefits which are being poured upon us. I should also like to pay this tribute to the force under Brigadier Snow which liberated us and which is now assisting to rehabilitate us. There exists between that force and the people of the Channel Islands the most wonderful cordiality and goodwill and that again is a bond of friendship and union with the Mother Country which Channel Islanders will never forget. My last word of greeting must be to the Channel Islanders who are still waiting as we are, for reunion. I should like to send a special word to those people who were deported from our shores, to the men and women of Laufen, of Wurzach and of Biberach and to the many prisoners-of-war from the Channel Islands who are awaiting return to their island and to reunion with us. Believe me, everything possible is being done, both in London and here to expedite the moment of reunion. It will come as soon as it is safely possible to do so.

And I know that you, Channel Islanders who are pining for return, will realise that it is only one short month ago since this island was in German occupation, that an enormous work lies ahead for Brigadier Snow and his force, to clear the island of all its unwelcome Germans and all that they left behind in the way of mines, displaced persons, and many other factors which have to be cleared up before the island is really once more itself. And when I talk to you of that hour of reunion which lies ahead may I just give this word of warning. You may find things somewhat changed when you come back. I know that Channel Islanders will remember, when they think in terms of coming back to their island home, of the conditions which have existed here during the five unhappy years of German occupation.

But perhaps I should try to remind you of some of the factors which have altered us a little. We have read no new books, we have seen no new films, we have read no newspapers and we have not received from you or from any other part of the world any letters except 25 word Red Cross messages during five years. And, perhaps most of all, for years past now, we have been cut off from all listening to the radio. When I say 'all listening' you will understand that we have constantly kept in touch with the broadcasts of the BBC. But try to imagine the conditions under which we have listened: in holes and corners, behind closed doors, off radio sets very often hidden in the thick recesses of our Guernsey and Jersey granite walls. We were able to listen at risk of imprisonment, but we had obviously to listen for the shortest time possible. The brave people who listened took down, as well as they could, what they had heard and circulated the news.

That is the sort of background of our minds, minds which during five years of German domination have been cut off from all contacts with the outside world; and at the same time flooded with every form of pernicious German propaganda. But they never really succeeded in sinking our spirit. Then think also of the different conditions which exist in the island. In 1940, when you left us, we were all set for our ordinary potato, tomato and visitor season. Then came the German occupation.

In the winter of 1940 we in Jersey turned over to the growing of wheat. Our old water power mills, which will be familiar to you, with such names as Quétivel, Tesson, Gargate, Malasie, Baxter, all these mills were reconditioned, and in those mills we have ground in these years all the wheat that we grew in the island, all the wheat that was necessary to make our daily bread. As you know so well our shops, in 1940, were full of everything that money could buy. They have been absolutely sucked dry. The Germans bought everything, with their bad money, which was for sale. We were absolutely left bare. We sent a buying commission to France to buy what we could buy. We had no banking facilities, at least not until nearly the very end. We had to send our money across in suitcases, pile them up in ordinary cupboards in our office in Granville and pay in cash for everything which we bought. The factory at Summerland was placed at our disposal and there we improvised the manufacture of clothing and footwear. We went in as far as we possibly could, for communal feeding. The Sun Works at First Tower were turned over to the manufacture of soup. As far as we possibly could we managed to feed, to clothe and to house the population in all these improvised ways.

All that continued until D-Day. D-Day brought to us a wonderful hope of approaching liberation, but also problems of the greatest magnitude, because our source of supply in France was cut off. It was no longer possible to buy meat, or textiles, or footwear, or medicines, or all the 1001 things we had been buying before. From that time onward, conditions in this island, and indeed in all the Channel Islands really became serious. Our supply of gas failed in the month of September. We had no coal, everyone had to cook as best they might on little fires made up of twigs of wood. We bought out or took over bakeries all over the island and built bakers' ovens of our own and in these ovens we cooked such meals as we had. It meant going down in the morning with your pot of vegetables to the oven and fetching it at dinner time with your meal cooked. Later on electricity failed. The lucky people had perhaps a few candles or a little oil. Others had nothing whatsoever; the only way that was open to them was to go to bed as soon as the light failed.

Conditions gradually got worse. But the Red Cross, that wonderful ship Vega came and saved us from undoubted destruction. No words of mine could possibly pay tribute to the wonderful work that has been done by the British and International Red Cross in saving the Channel Islands in that way.

Family Reunion

My father wrote to all the family as soon as postal services were restored. On 15th May he wrote on an official post paid card which was provided to the inhabitants to contact their relatives. It was headed: "REOCCUPATION OF CHANNEL ISLANDS. This card is liable to CENSORSHIP and may be sent only to an address in the BRITISH EMPIRE or to a member of HM Forces."

On 20th May he wrote more fully. These letters, reread after more than fifty years, seem to bring out his gentleness and strength in an amazing way:

My dear Michael

What a thrill to see your writing again after all these years. It hasn't changed a lot and I recognised it at once.

It doesn't really seem like five years since that grim day you left Jersey. The first four years went like a flash, but since D Day it has seemed interminable. We expected to be relieved at once and we used to go out to the north of the island watching the battle draw nearer and nearer. Then it began to recede as they got round the Bay of St. Malo. But we still thought the Germans would get out. It seemed madness to us to lock up 15,000 troops in a little island when they would have been invaluable over there.

Well, our only consolation was that we did - through no effort of our own, keep these troops out of the fight. Of course the island was immensely strong. I haven't yet seen the inside of the forts, but the officers tell me they were immense. The whole place has been tunnelled and there are huge galleries and underground forts all over the place. One goes from St. Peter's Valley under our hill.

I never thought for one moment we could lose. I little knew how weak we were. Singapore, Tobruk and Crete gave us shocks. I think Crete shook me more than anything. It seemed impossible that they could take it from the air alone.

For the last three years we had to listen in secret. I kept my set, a small one, under my pillow. When the hunt became hot we hid it in a dustbin in the ground outside the kitchen window and only brought it in at night. One day a German officer caught me going upstairs to listen in, but he came about billeting and didn't search. Another time they searched the house for an escaped Russian and I stripped the bed and flung the clothes over it as if it hadn't been made. A week after they looked for the Russian, I took him in and hid him for a week in the spare bedroom. He was a parachutist and couldn't speak a word of English. Then I had to find another place for him, as Mrs. Newbery [Mrs. Lock] fell sick and had to go into hospital.

We have had a few excitements I will tell you about some day, but it has mostly been very dull - but always the tension and shadow of the Gestapo [sic.] over us. You never knew whom you could trust, as they had many informers. It was like being in a world of Edgar Wallace, or Valentine Williams. But it is extraordinary how easily you get accustomed to it and ignore it - though it is there underneath all the time…

I don't know when I shall come over - soon I hope as I am very tired - but travel is going to be difficult for a few weeks. However, I have several good reasons for priority - five to be precise - and will worry people until they let me go.

Just over a month later he 'phoned my mother to say that he was coming over the next day. She wrote to me at school:

He is leaving tonight [26th June] and arriving at Southampton at 6 am - just as we did. I'll be meeting him at Yeovil Junction at 12.5. No plans yet. I don't even know how long he has got, but it's likely that we'll get to you the weekend after next.

Together they went round to our various boarding schools to see us. Both he and we felt enormously the burden of the years that had passed. He had last seen me aged 12; I was now 17, an enormous difference! To me he seemed so much older, thin and haggard. The five years of loneliness and deprivation had undoubtedly taken their toll. On his return he wrote about our meeting:

It was marvellous to see you again after all these years. I'm afraid I was rather shaken at first because you had changed so much. You see, it has not seemed like five years to me, because I never gave up hope and always saw relief round the corner. So when I saw how grown up you were, the whole weight of those five years seemed to fall upon me suddenly.

I hope this letter arrives to wish you good luck in your exam. Perhaps now that you feel that you have not the whole responsibility for the future of the family, your mind will be at rest.

On 23rd August, at the end of our school summer term, more than three months after the Liberation, Anthony and I met our sister Daphne, and stayed overnight at St. Thomas's Hospital. We caught the airport coach from Victoria Coach Station to Croydon from where we flew back to Jersey, by the newly restored Channel Islands Airways. We resumed our life at home, five years, two months and five days after our departure.

My father had thought of everything. He had already bought a second car, the little green Austin 7, and announced that we could have it for our own use, and he would arrange for me to have driving lessons. Anthony followed me as soon as he was sixteen and the others in due course.

My father had been souvenir hunting for us and duly passed on to us: a photograph of Adolf Hitler (from the *Feldkommandantur* in College House), a bombing map of Greater London and London Docks, with targets outlined (from the *Luftwaffe* headquarters on Mont Cambrai), four steel helmets, a rifle (with a broken butt which was why he did not hand it in), a bayonet in its scabbard, copies of the *Evening Post* containing the orders of the *Kommandant* at the start of the Occupation, and one of the *Bilderbogen* books published by Baron von Aufsess.

We also went souvenir hunting in the German bunkers, but most people had got there before us, and all I found were heaps of books from the German Army Bookshop *'Heeresbücherei'*, distributed by the *Frontbuchhandllung*, which was installed in the pre-war 'Fifty-Shilling Tailors' in St. Helier. Some of these came in useful for my studies of German literature.

Chapter 14

Epilogue

The mines were cleared, the ammunition removed from the bunkers, the larger guns dumped over the cliffs at Les Landes, the railway lines dismantled, and the tunnels sealed off; and life in Jersey gradually returned to normal. Swimming and surfing began again, more hardcore was placed on the tennis court, the surface was completed and we began to play there. Jersey began to recover something of its pre-war appearance, but many scars, physical, mental and spiritual, remained to be healed.

I had registered for National Service, but due to my Jersey residence was not called up. I went to Oxford to study languages and then teaching and on to ordination. I worked in England before going to the British Embassy in Bonn, returning to Jersey as Rector of St. Brelade. My brother Anthony went to Cambridge to study medicine and into general practice in Jersey. Our sister Daphne went to study orthopaedic nursing in Oxford and, briefly physiotherapy at St. Thomas's Hospital. My brother Richard went to Cambridge to study veterinary surgery. Our careers took us briefly abroad, mine to Germany; Anthony's to Dublin, Barbados and back to Jersey; our sister Daphne married her husband Brian and went with him to Aden, Hong Kong and Malaya, where the British fought a successful campaign against the Communist insurgency and secured the peaceful future of the Malaysian Federation. Richard's career as a veterinary surgeon and professor took him to the United States, Scotland, and worldwide.

My father eventually got the holiday he had been dreaming about since his letter in 1940. In May, 1948 he and my mother went to Grindelwald in Switzerland. He wrote:

My dear Michael,

During those grim war years, this holiday was one of my dreams. Even before that we used to talk about it, but it was always impossible. The house had to be paid for or we had to look for schools or something. Realization has brought no disappointment. We are enjoying every minute of it, at least I am and I think Mum is in her quiet way.

I love this country with its trim chalets and neat curtained windows. The people are so courteous without being in any way servile, and they are so genuinely glad to see us. The countryman rarely fails to give you his greeting 'Grüss Gott' which is so much nicer than 'Guten Tag', and shows their unspoilt simplicity. I cannot help comparing their attitude with that of some rapacious Jerseymen who are only out for what they can get. The people want us to come to their country not only because it is their livelihood but because they are proud of it and want to show it to us. In the cafés for example- and we have been to several - the girls don't hang about for a tip but hurry away, almost with indecent haste; they know we are poor and they don't mind.

There is an excellent café here, rather an imposing one and Madame is equally imposing - a fat cheerful looking woman. During the course of a conversation she prefaced a remark - 'when I was in service' and said it in no apologetic tone. Although she is now well-to-do she is not ashamed of having been in service. I don't think an English woman in her position would have been as frank - which shows I think a true sense of values. An amusing thing happened. They have a gramophone and I asked for 'Lili Marlene' [a song sung by German singer Lale Andersen from

Radio Belgrade for the benefit of the German Afrika Korps, but regularly listened to by the British Eighth Army in the desert]. Madame brightened up at once and said: 'Do you mind it because some of the English looked rather angry when I used to play it so I put it away.' I said: 'No, I like it, because it's a good tune.'

I got a lot of interesting side lines on the war from her, and I'm sure she is genuinely pro-British. She said they knew what was happening in Germany (the atrocities etc.) before we did. I asked her what they thought in 1940 and she said that apart from a few Swiss Nazis, they all knew we would come out on top because we always do.

When we came I'm afraid I was a bit too enthusiastic about the walking and got Mum rather tired: she gets very out of breath climbing. So now we have a long day followed by a quiet one.

The alpine flowers are marvellous and grow in far greater profusion than I ever imagined - large areas blue with gentian or pink with primula. The scenery is of course superb and one uses superlatives for so many ordinary things that it is difficult to find words to describe it.

At the end of the Occupation my father was not yet fifty years of age, and he had over fifteen years to run in his career as a surgeon. Though exhausted in body and mind, he did not rest on his laurels, and he soon addressed the task of bringing his much loved hospital up-to-date. As a colleague wrote:

For many people these [war] years alone would have drained their energies, but after the war Arthur Halliwell played a great part in transforming the Hospital into a modern up-to-date hospital of which the island can be justly proud. First the new Nurses' Home, which enabled a flourishing Nurses' Training School to be established, then building up the consultant staff, and finally the New North Wing with its ultra modern operating suite - the envy of most hospitals in England.

My father retired in 1961, selling the house in St. Peter and moving to St. Ouen, where he and my mother converted a cottage and set about the huge task of creating another garden. He died on 8th September 1966, and my mother on 14th May 1972. They are both buried in the cemetery at St. Ouen's Church.

At his funeral, a long standing friend, the Revd Geoffrey Baker, spoke of ACH's "outstanding gifts in the field of medicine and surgery… and warm and accepting humanity." He also referred to "another, inner side of him, which fewer have known about. This is the inner, spiritual side, the powerhouse from which his abundantly gifted life received its driving force. Inside a frail seeming frame, burnt a fire of immense power. It would be difficult to have ever met him and not been conscious of this great strength of spirit, which visibly shone out of him. His most alert mind, his questing intellect, were allied to a very great and uncompromising honesty. Not for him acceptance just because it would be easy, or because others accepted. His ever present belief in God was too big and powerful a thing to be pinned down easily or quickly into any particular creed - it was certainly far too great to be confined within any small sect or party. It led him finally to the truth about God which lies in his son Jesus Christ… finding in our Lord the key which unlocks the whole mystery of our universe."

When the extension to the Jersey General Hospital was constructed in the 1970s, a new lecture theatre was named 'The Halliwell Lecture Theatre' in memory of my father's work in the Island, and in particular his work during the Occupation in the field of the training of nurses and doctors. I unveiled a plaque at the entrance to the theatre reading:

THE HALLIWELL LECTURE THEATRE.

THIS LECTURE THEATRE IS NAMED IN MEMORY

OF MR A. C. HALLIWELL, CONSULTANT SURGEON

AT THE GENERAL HOSPITAL BETWEEN 1932 AND 1961.

IT WAS OFFICIALLY OPENED ON 2ND MAY 1980

Many years later the theatre was comprehensively refurbished, and in 2003 a new plaque, complete with a photograph of ACH, replaced the former one. It reads:

ARTHUR CLARE HALLIWELL

(1896 - 1966)

CONSULTANT SURGEON

JERSEY GENERAL HOSPITAL

(1932 - 1961)

MR HALLIWELL, WIDELY KNOWN AS "A.C.H." WAS APPOINTED CONSULTANT SURGEON IN

JERSEY IN 1932. IN JUNE 1940, HAVING SENT HIS FAMILY TO ENGLAND, HE REMAINED AT

HIS POST AND PROVIDED THE CORE OF MEDICAL SERVICES AT THE GENERAL HOSPITAL

THROUGHOUT THE GERMAN OCCUPATION. IN ADDITION TO PERFORMING THE TOTAL RANGE

OF SURGICAL PROCEDURES, IN DIFFICULT AND DETERIORATING CIRCUMSTANCES,

HE SUPPORTED ENDEAVOURS TO TRAIN LOCAL NURSES. HE SUPERVISED AND

ENCOURAGED A NUMBER OF PROSPECTIVE MEDICAL STUDENTS, WHO HAD BEEN FORCED

TO REMAIN IN JERSEY, THEY SUBSEQUENTLY

COMPLETED THEIR MEDICAL TRAINING AFTER THE OCCUPATION. DURING THE POST-WAR

PERIOD HE PLAYED A MAJOR ROLE IN TRANSFORMING THE HOSPITAL INTO A MODERN,

UP-TO-DATE FACILITY, CULMINATING IN THE PLANNING OF THE 1960'S WING.

THE ADJACENT LECTURE THEATRE WAS NAMED AFTER MR HALLIWELL IN RECOGNITION

OF HIS SIGNIFICANT

CONTRIBUTION, PARTICULARLY AS A TEACHER AND LECTURER TO NURSING AND MEDICAL

STUDENTS AND ALSO TO THE HOSPITAL COMMUNITY AND MEDICAL LIFE IN JERSEY

OVER ALMOST THIRTY YEARS.